Contents

MW01703431

© Harcourt Achieve Inc. All rights reserved.

Features

The *Practical Science* series will help children succeed in science. Science concepts are presented through engaging, easy-to-implement experiments using materials readily available at home, school, or local stores. After completing the series, children will be armed with the concepts and confidence they need to achieve at a higher level in science class and on standardized tests.

Practical Science: Standards-Based Science Experiments, Grades 1–2 contains 3 units: Physical Science, Life Science, and Earth Science. Each unit is divided into 4 lessons. The content of all 12 lessons is based upon National Science Education Standards (NSES) and the Full Option Science System (FOSS) Modules for Grades 1–2.

Tables on pages 4–5 provide a correlation between each lesson and the NSES standards and FOSS Modules.

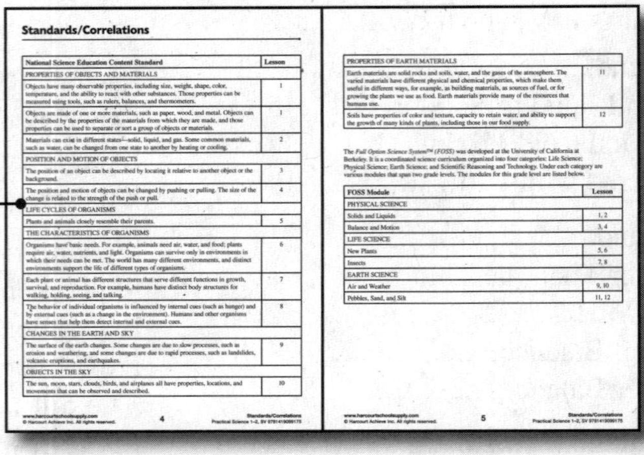

Standards/Correlations

National Science Education Content Standard	Lesson
PROPERTIES OF OBJECTS AND MATERIALS	
Objects have many observable properties, including size, weight, shape, color, temperature, and the ability to react with other substances. Those properties can be measured using tools, such as rulers, balances, and thermometers.	1
Objects are made of one or more materials, such as paper, wood, and metal. Objects can be described by the properties of the materials from which they are made, and those properties can be used to separate or sort a group of objects or materials.	1
Materials can exist in different states—solid, liquid, and gas. Some common materials, such as water, can be changed from one state to another by heating or cooling.	2
POSITION AND MOTION OF OBJECTS	
The position of an object can be described by locating it relative to another object or the background.	3
The position and motion of objects can be changed by pushing or pulling. The size of the change is related to the strength of the push or pull.	4
LIFE CYCLES OF ORGANISMS	
Plants and animals closely resemble their parents.	5
THE CHARACTERISTICS OF ORGANISMS	
Organisms have basic needs. For example, animals need air, water, and food; plants require air, water, nutrients, and light. Organisms can survive only in environments in which their needs can be met. The world has many different environments, and distinct environments support the life of different types of organisms.	6
Each plant or animal has different structures that serve different functions in growth, survival, and reproduction. For example, humans have distinct body structures for walking, holding, seeing, and talking.	7
The behavior of individual organisms is influenced by internal cues (such as hunger) and by external cues (such as a change in the environment). Humans and other organisms have senses that help them detect internal and external cues.	8
CHANGES IN THE EARTH AND SKY	
The surface of the earth changes. Some changes are due to slow processes, such as erosion and weathering, and some changes are due to rapid processes, such as landslides, volcanic eruptions, and earthquakes.	9
OBJECTS IN THE SKY	
The sun, moon, stars, clouds, birds, and airplanes all have properties, locations, and movements that can be observed and described.	10

www.harcourtschoolsupply.com © Harcourt Achieve Inc. All rights reserved. 4 Standards/Correlations Practical Science 1–2, SV 9781419099175

PROPERTIES OF EARTH MATERIALS	
Earth materials are solid rocks and soils, water, and the gases of the atmosphere. The varied materials have different physical and chemical properties, which make them useful in different ways, for example, as building materials, as sources of fuel, or for growing the plants we use as food. Earth materials provide many of the resources that humans use.	11
Soils have properties of color and texture, capacity to retain water, and ability to support the growth of many kinds of plants, including those in our food supply.	12

The *Full Option Science System*™ (FOSS) was developed at the University of California at Berkeley. It is a coordinated science curriculum organized into four categories: Life Science; Physical Science; Earth Science; and Scientific Reasoning and Technology. Under each category are various modules that span two grade levels. The modules for this grade level are listed below.

FOSS Module	Lesson
PHYSICAL SCIENCE	
Solids and Liquids	1, 2
Balance and Motion	3, 4
LIFE SCIENCE	
New Plants	5, 6
Insects	7, 8
EARTH SCIENCE	
Air and Weather	9, 10
Pebbles, Sand, and Silt	11, 12

www.harcourtschoolsupply.com © Harcourt Achieve Inc. All rights reserved. 5 Standards/Correlations Practical Science 1–2, SV 9781419099175

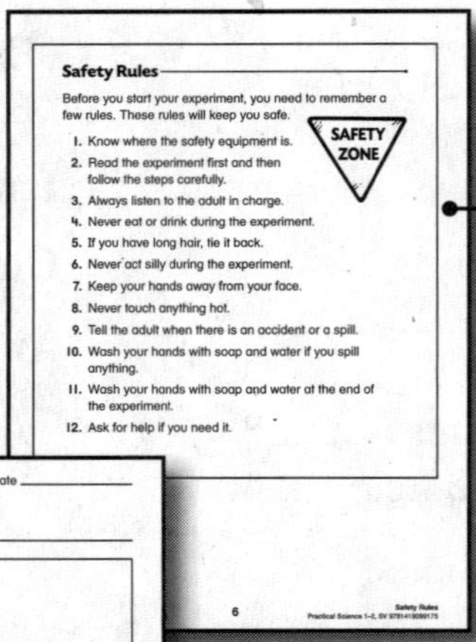

Safety Rules

Before you start your experiment, you need to remember a few rules. These rules will keep you safe.

1. Know where the safety equipment is.
2. Read the experiment first and then follow the steps carefully.
3. Always listen to the adult in charge.
4. Never eat or drink during the experiment.
5. If you have long hair, tie it back.
6. Never act silly during the experiment.
7. Keep your hands away from your face.
8. Never touch anything hot.
9. Tell the adult when there is an accident or a spill.
10. Wash your hands with soap and water if you spill anything.
11. Wash your hands with soap and water at the end of the experiment.
12. Ask for help if you need it.

6 Safety Rules Practical Science 1–2, SV 9781419099175

A Safety Rules sheet provides safety rules for children to review before beginning each experiment. The Safety Rules sheet can be posted in the classroom or included in children's science folders or journals for easy reference.

A blank Lab Sheet is provided on page 92. This Lab Sheet can be used during the experiments within the *Practical Science* series, and it can be utilized for other experiments.

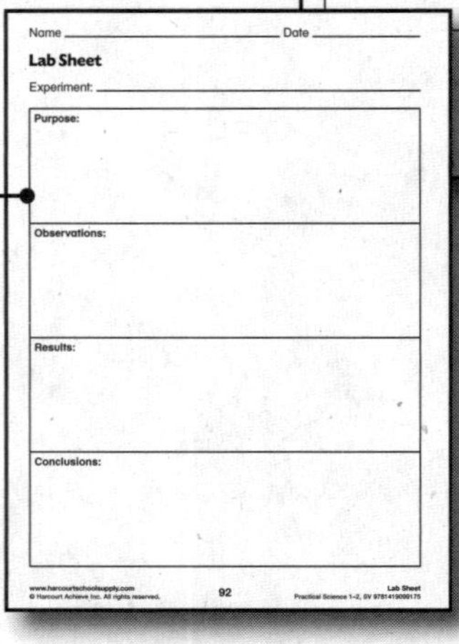

Name ______ Date ______

Lab Sheet

Experiment: ______

Purpose:

Observations:

Results:

Conclusions:

www.harcourtschoolsupply.com © Harcourt Achieve Inc. All rights reserved. 92 Lab Sheet Practical Science 1–2, SV 9781419099175

© Harcourt Achieve Inc. All rights reserved.

The Lessons begin on page 7. Each lesson consists of a Background page followed by 3 experiments. While the lessons are written for the child, it is advised that the teacher or parent walk the child through the background and experiments to ensure understanding.

The Background provides a summary of the main concepts covered in the lesson. It includes key vocabulary words in boldface, which are fully defined in the Glossary on pages 93–94.

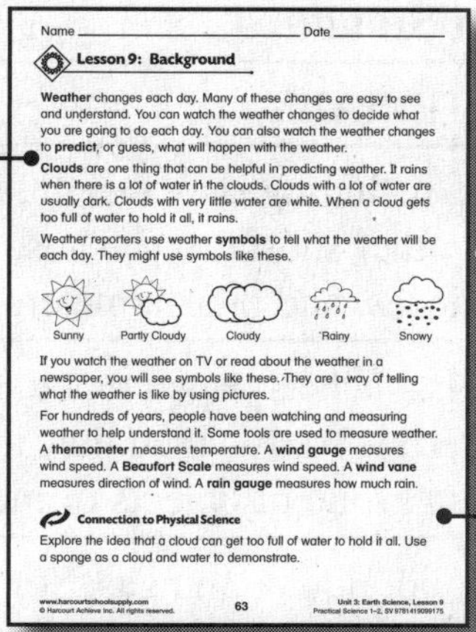

Name __________ Date __________

Lesson 9: Background

Weather changes each day. Many of these changes are easy to see and understand. You can watch the weather changes to decide what you are going to do each day. You can also watch the weather changes to **predict**, or guess, what will happen with the weather.

Clouds are one thing that can be helpful in predicting weather. It rains when there is a lot of water in the clouds. Clouds with a lot of water are usually dark. Clouds with very little water are white. When a cloud gets too full of water to hold it all, it rains.

Weather reporters use weather **symbols** to tell what the weather will be each day. They might use symbols like these.

Sunny Partly Cloudy Cloudy Rainy Snowy

If you watch the weather on TV or read about the weather in a newspaper, you will see symbols like these. They are a way of telling what the weather is like by using pictures.

For hundreds of years, people have been watching and measuring weather to help understand it. Some tools are used to measure weather. A **thermometer** measures temperature. A **wind gauge** measures wind speed. A **Beaufort Scale** measures wind speed. A **wind vane** measures direction of wind. A **rain gauge** measures how much rain.

Connection to Physical Science

Explore the idea that a cloud can get too full of water to hold it all. Use a sponge as a cloud and water to demonstrate.

www.harcourtschoolsupply.com
© Harcourt Achieve Inc. All rights reserved. 63 Unit 3: Earth Science, Lesson 9
Practical Science 1–2, SV 9781419099175

The Background pages include a connection to another area of science. These activities involve critical thinking. Activities involving writing should be completed on another sheet of paper.

A Materials list details all required materials. Room is given so that children can place a check mark by each item.

Each experiment begins with a Purpose. This explains the focus of the experiment and what will be done.

The Procedure provides step-by-step instructions to complete the experiment.

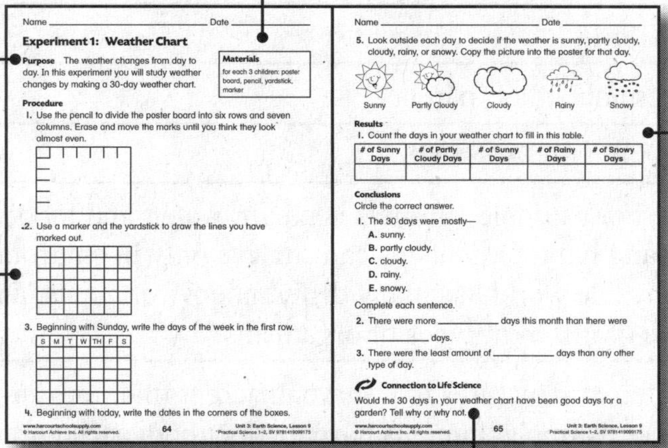

Name __________ Date __________

Experiment 1: Weather Chart

Purpose The weather changes from day to day. In this experiment you will study weather changes by making a 30-day weather chart.

Materials
for each 3 children: poster board, pencil, yardstick, marker

Procedure

1. Use the pencil to divide the poster board into six rows and seven columns. Erase and move the marks until you think they look almost even.
2. Use a marker and the yardstick to draw the lines you have marked out.
3. Beginning with Sunday, write the days of the week in the first row.

S	M	T	W	TH	F	S

4. Beginning with today, write the dates in the corners of the boxes.

www.harcourtschoolsupply.com
© Harcourt Achieve Inc. All rights reserved. 64 Unit 3: Earth Science, Lesson 9
Practical Science 1–2, SV 9781419099175

Name __________ Date __________

5. Look outside each day to decide if the weather is sunny, partly cloudy, cloudy, rainy, or snowy. Copy the picture into the poster for that day.

Sunny Partly Cloudy Cloudy Rainy Snowy

Results

1. Count the days in your weather chart to fill in this table.

# of Sunny Days	# of Partly Cloudy Days	# of Sunny Days	# of Rainy Days	# of Snowy Days

Conclusions

Circle the correct answer.

1. The 30 days were mostly—
   A. sunny.
   B. partly cloudy.
   C. cloudy.
   D. rainy.
   E. snowy.

Complete each sentence.

2. There were more ________ days this month than there were ________ days.
3. There were the least amount of ________ days than any other type of day.

Connection to Life Science

Would the 30 days in your weather chart have been good days for a garden? Tell why or why not.

www.harcourtschoolsupply.com
© Harcourt Achieve Inc. All rights reserved. 65 Unit 3: Earth Science, Lesson 9
Practical Science 1–2, SV 9781419099175

The child will complete the Results and Conclusions upon finishing the experiment. This section will help you check for understanding and can lead into a discussion, especially when children have varied results. Answers to the Conclusions are found in the Answer Key on pages 95–96.

Most experiments include a Connection to another area of science. As in the Background, these activities help children think critically about the science topic. Activities involving writing should be completed on another sheet of paper.

The experiments presented in this book can be used to introduce, review, or extend science concepts. In addition, they may also be used as a basis for a more in-depth project, such as for a science fair. In this case, the child should locate additional information about the topic from books or the Internet.

Science is about discovery and exploration. The experiments in the *Practical Science* series will provide children with ample opportunity to discover and explore scientific concepts. Through this process, science will become exciting and interesting.

© Harcourt Achieve Inc. All rights reserved.

Standards/Correlations

National Science Education Content Standard	Lesson
PROPERTIES OF OBJECTS AND MATERIALS	
Objects have many observable properties, including size, weight, shape, color, temperature, and the ability to react with other substances. Those properties can be measured using tools, such as rulers, balances, and thermometers.	1
Objects are made of one or more materials, such as paper, wood, and metal. Objects can be described by the properties of the materials from which they are made, and those properties can be used to separate or sort a group of objects or materials.	1
Materials can exist in different states—solid, liquid, and gas. Some common materials, such as water, can be changed from one state to another by heating or cooling.	2
POSITION AND MOTION OF OBJECTS	
The position of an object can be described by locating it relative to another object or the background.	3
The position and motion of objects can be changed by pushing or pulling. The size of the change is related to the strength of the push or pull.	4
LIFE CYCLES OF ORGANISMS	
Plants and animals closely resemble their parents.	5
THE CHARACTERISTICS OF ORGANISMS	
Organisms have basic needs. For example, animals need air, water, and food; plants require air, water, nutrients, and light. Organisms can survive only in environments in which their needs can be met. The world has many different environments, and distinct environments support the life of different types of organisms.	6
Each plant or animal has different structures that serve different functions in growth, survival, and reproduction. For example, humans have distinct body structures for walking, holding, seeing, and talking.	7
The behavior of individual organisms is influenced by internal cues (such as hunger) and by external cues (such as a change in the environment). Humans and other organisms have senses that help them detect internal and external cues.	8
CHANGES IN THE EARTH AND SKY	
The surface of the earth changes. Some changes are due to slow processes, such as erosion and weathering, and some changes are due to rapid processes, such as landslides, volcanic eruptions, and earthquakes.	9
OBJECTS IN THE SKY	
The sun, moon, stars, clouds, birds, and airplanes all have properties, locations, and movements that can be observed and described.	10

© Harcourt Achieve Inc. All rights reserved.

PROPERTIES OF EARTH MATERIALS	
Earth materials are solid rocks and soils, water, and the gases of the atmosphere. The varied materials have different physical and chemical properties, which make them useful in different ways, for example, as building materials, as sources of fuel, or for growing the plants we use as food. Earth materials provide many of the resources that humans use.	11
Soils have properties of color and texture, capacity to retain water, and ability to support the growth of many kinds of plants, including those in our food supply.	12

The *Full Option Science System™ (FOSS)* was developed at the University of California at Berkeley. It is a coordinated science curriculum organized into four categories: Life Science; Physical Science; Earth Science; and Scientific Reasoning and Technology. Under each category are various modules that span two grade levels. The modules for this grade level are listed below.

FOSS Module	**Lesson**
PHYSICAL SCIENCE	
Solids and Liquids	1, 2
Balance and Motion	3, 4
LIFE SCIENCE	
New Plants	5, 6
Insects	7, 8
EARTH SCIENCE	
Air and Weather	9, 10
Pebbles, Sand, and Silt	11, 12

© Harcourt Achieve Inc. All rights reserved.

Safety Rules

Before you start your experiment, you need to remember a few rules. These rules will keep you safe.

1. Know where the safety equipment is.
2. Read the experiment first and then follow the steps carefully.
3. Always listen to the adult in charge.
4. Never eat or drink during the experiment.
5. If you have long hair, tie it back.
6. Never act silly during the experiment.
7. Keep your hands away from your face.
8. Never touch anything hot.
9. Tell the adult when there is an accident or a spill.
10. Wash your hands with soap and water if you spill anything.
11. Wash your hands with soap and water at the end of the experiment.
12. Ask for help if you need it.

© Harcourt Achieve Inc. All rights reserved.

Name ______________________________ Date ______________

Lesson 1: Background

Look at the world around you. Everything you see is matter. **Matter** is anything that has **mass** and takes up space. Matter is found in **nature**.

When you look at matter, you can see its properties. A **property** describes an object. You can tell what color or shape it is. You can tell if it is smooth or rough. You can use this information to tell others about it.

You can also look at many objects and know what material they are made of. It is easy to tell what these things are made of:

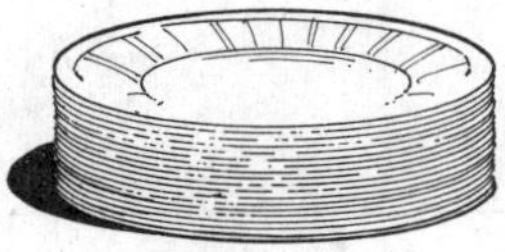
Paper

Plastic

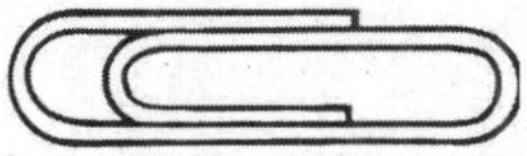
Metal

Wood

By knowing what objects are made of, you can think of ways to use the objects. Look at the table for some examples.

Object	How it can be used
Paper	To write on To make into books and other reading material
Plastic	To make microwaveable containers To make shampoo bottles
Metal	To make car parts To make computer parts
Wood	To make pencils To build houses

Connection to Earth Science

Find out how long objects made of wood, plastic, metal, and paper can be underground without falling apart.

© Harcourt Achieve Inc. All rights reserved.

Name ______________________ Date ____________

Experiment 1: Is It Green, Square, or Round?

Materials
objects in the room that are green, square, round, smooth, and large

Purpose You can describe things by how they look, feel, and touch. You will find things that match descriptions.

Procedure

1. Find things in the classroom to complete the Results Tables.
2. Name things that could fit in other groups. Write their names in the Conclusions Table.

Results

3 green things	3 square things	3 round things
1. 2. 3.	1. 2. 3.	1. 2. 3.

3 smooth things	3 large things
1. 2. 3.	1. 2. 3.

© Harcourt Achieve Inc. All rights reserved.

Name ______________________ Date ____________

Conclusions

Things That Could Fit in Other Groups		
From this group	**One thing that could fit in another group**	**Another group it could fit in**
Green Things		
Square Things		
Round Things		
Smooth Things		
Large Things		

Write the answers.

1. List a thing that is blue. ______________________
2. List a thing that is round. ______________________
3. List a thing that is both blue and round. ______________________

Connection to Earth Science

Look in a book or go outside to look at rocks, dirt, and clouds. Think of two words to describe each of them.

© Harcourt Achieve Inc. All rights reserved.

Name ______________________ Date ____________

Experiment 2: Sorting Objects by Descriptions

Purpose You can look at things to see how they are alike and different. You can then use this information to sort the objects into groups.

Materials	about 40 different red, blue, and green objects, such as 3 of each of the following: pencils, plastic rulers, plastic cups, wooden rulers, wooden blocks, sheets of paper, index cards, paper airplanes, plastic spoons, stickers, plastic chips, wooden dowel rods, keys, metal paper clips, paper clamps

Procedure and Results

1. Study the objects.
2. Sort the objects into three groups by color. Give each group a name that tells what is in the group, such as Green Group. Write the number of objects in each group.

	Group 1	Group 2	Group 3
Name			
# of objects			

3. Sort the objects into three groups by size. Give each group a name that tells what is in the group, such as Large Group. Write the number of objects in each group.

	Group 1	Group 2	Group 3
Name			
# of objects			

4. Sort the objects into three groups by materials they are made of. Give each group a name that tells what is in the group, such as Wooden Group. Write the number of objects in each group.

© Harcourt Achieve Inc. All rights reserved.

Name ______________________ Date ____________

	Group 1	Group 2	Group 3
Name			
# of objects			

Conclusions

Answer the questions.

1. Which of the three sorts was the easiest to do? Explain why.

____

____

2. Which of the three sorts was the hardest to do? Explain why.

____

____

3. Which of the three sorts would be most useful if you were choosing things to leave outside? Explain why.

____

____

4. Which of the three sorts would be most useful if you were choosing things to place in a small box? Explain why.

____

____

Connection to Life Science

Make the following lists of things you can see in nature: three red things, three small things, and three things with feathers.

© Harcourt Achieve Inc. All rights reserved.

Name ______________________ Date ____________

Experiment 3: What Is It Made Of?

Materials

pencil
wooden block
plastic spoon
index card
metal paper clip
stainless steel spoon
wooden ruler
plastic ruler
sheet of paper
sticker
key

Purpose You can learn about an object by knowing what it is made of. You will study objects to explore what they are made of.

Procedure

1. Sort the objects by what they are made of.
2. Write the names of the objects in the first Results Table.
3. In the next Results Table, circle the word or words that describe each group.

Results

Wood	Plastic	Paper	Metal

	Bends?	Supports?	Can Tear, Break, or Chip?
Wood	Easily Sometimes Not at all	Strongly A little Not at all	Yes No
Plastic	Easily Sometimes Not at all	Strongly A little Not at all	Yes No

© Harcourt Achieve Inc. All rights reserved.

Name ______________________________ Date ______________

	Bends?	Supports?	Can Tear, Break, or Chip?
Paper	Easily Sometimes Not at all	Strongly A little Not at all	Yes No
Metal	Easily Sometimes Not at all	Strongly A little Not at all	Yes No

Conclusions

Complete each sentence.

1. A spoon would not be made of paper because ______________________________.
2. A key would not be made of wood because ______________________________.
3. Everyday silverware would not be made of plastic because ______________________________.

Connection to Life Science

Two of the groups of objects you have sorted are made from trees. Which two are they? What are two other things made from trees?

© Harcourt Achieve Inc. All rights reserved.

Name ______________________ Date ______________

Lesson 2: Background

Matter can be a **liquid** like water, a **solid** like a desk, or **gas** like air.

Liquids, solids, and gases can be in different forms.

Liquids

A watery liquid moves around like water. It doesn't hold its shape when poured. Examples are milk, coffee, and gasoline.

A thick liquid moves like glue or runny pudding. When it is poured, it holds some of its shape. Some examples are honey and oil.

Solids

A solid is not runny at all. It holds its shape. Examples are an apple, a brick, and a coffee cup.

A solid can be mixed with a liquid. In this case, you have a **mixture** of some solid and some liquid. Examples include soup, salsa, and ice water.

Solids that are left in soil may begin to **decay**, or fall apart. When things decay, they become part of the soil.

Gases

A gas is not a solid or a liquid. It is like air. You cannot see it. It takes the shape of the container it is in.

In these experiments, you will create mixtures. You will also work with water that **evaporates**, or turns into a gas.

Connection to Life Science

Many fruits and vegetables are solids that, when squeezed, give off a liquid. List at least five fruits and vegetables that do this.

© Harcourt Achieve Inc. All rights reserved.

Name ______________________________ Date ______________

Experiment 1: From Liquid to Solid to Gas

Purpose When you heat or cool something, it changes. You will change things by freezing and heating them.

Materials

adult helper

3 small paper cups half full of water

3 microwave-safe bowls

3 scoops (about 2 tablespoons each) of ice cream in 3 microwave-safe plastic bowls

3 eggs broken into 3 microwave-safe plastic bowls

freezer

microwave

fork

3 paper towels

hot plates

Procedure and Results

1. Place the half cups of water in a freezer overnight.
2. Take the cups out of the freezer.
3. Work with the ice in the paper cups.
   - Remove the ice cubes from the small paper cups.
   - Place each ice cube in a microwave-safe bowl.
   - Place two of the bowls in the freezer.
   - Place the other bowl on a desk or counter.
4. Work with the ice cream.
   - Place two bowls in the freezer.
   - Place one bowl on a desk or counter.
5. Work with the eggs.
   - Use the fork to whip the egg in each bowl.
   - Place one bowl in the freezer.
   - Place two bowls on a desk or counter.
6. Wait 45 minutes. Then fill in the first Results Table. Write <u>Watery liquid</u>; <u>Thick liquid</u>; <u>Some solid, some liquid</u>; <u>Solid</u>; or <u>Became a Gas</u> in the boxes in the three Results Tables.

	Ice	Ice Cream	Egg
Describe what you see on the desk or counter.			

© Harcourt Achieve Inc. All rights reserved.

Name ______________________ Date ____________

7. From the freezer, take one bowl with ice cream and one bowl with ice. Also take one bowl with egg from the desk or counter.
   - Cover each with a paper towel and place them in the microwave.
   - Cook them for 8 minutes, but stop and look at them every 2 minutes.
   - Have an adult helper remove the bowls from the microwave.
   - Fill in this Results Table.

	Describe after 2 minutes.	**Describe after 4 minutes.**	**Describe after 6 minutes.**	**Describe after 8 minutes.**
Ice				
Ice Cream				
Egg				

8. Take the last three bowls out of the freezer. Fill in this Results Table.

	Ice	**Ice Cream**	**Egg**
Describe after taking out of freezer.			

Conclusions

Circle the word that best completes each sentence.

1. Ice cream, water, and eggs are all (liquids, solids, gases) when they are frozen.
2. Ice cream, water, and eggs are (liquids, solids, gases) at room temperature.
3. Water is (liquid, solid, gas) after heating in the microwave for 8 minutes.
4. Heat makes an egg turn to (liquid, solid, gas).

Connection to Earth Science

Find how the water in this experiment relates to rain, snow, and hail.

© Harcourt Achieve Inc. All rights reserved.

Name ______________________________ Date ______________

Experiment 2: Hot and Cold Mixing

Materials

adult helper

2 cups hot water in a plastic bowl

2 cups cold water in a plastic bowl

2 paper cups each with $\frac{1}{4}$ cup sugar

2 paper cups each with $\frac{1}{4}$ cup peanut butter

2 paper cups each with 6 grapes

2 paper cups each with $\frac{1}{4}$ cup salt

2 paper cups each with $\frac{1}{4}$ cup ketchup

2 paper cups each with 4 saltine cracker squares

2 spoons

Purpose Many things mix into water. Some things mix easier with hot water than with cold water. You will explore how six different things mix with hot and cold water.

Procedure

1. Work with a partner.
2. At the same time:
   - One of you adds one of the paper cups of sugar to the hot water.
   - The other one of you adds one of the paper cups of sugar to the cold water.
3. Use spoons to stir until the sugar dissolves completely or until you see no more change taking place.
4. Complete the sugar column in the Results Table.
5. Repeat steps 2–5 for the peanut butter, grapes, salt, ketchup, and crackers.

Results

Write one of these numbers in each square:

1 (completely dissolves; result is a runny liquid)

2 (completely blends in; result is a thick liquid)

3 (some dissolves or blends; result is a liquid with some solid)

4 (does not dissolve or blend; result is a liquid and a solid)

© Harcourt Achieve Inc. All rights reserved.

Name ______________________________ Date ______________

	Sugar	Peanut Butter	Grapes	Salt	Ketchup	Crackers
						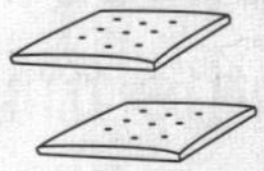
What happens when mixed with cold water?						
What happens when mixed with hot water?						

Conclusions

Circle the word or words that best complete each sentence.

1. It is (easier, harder) to mix most things in hot water than in cold water.
2. (Grapes, Crackers) did not mix at all with the hot or cold water.
3. The difference between a thick liquid and a liquid with some solids in it is that the thick liquid looks like (soup, one thing with no pieces showing).

Connection to Earth Science

If you pay attention, you can find liquids, solids, and liquid/solid combinations in nature. Make a list of two things in nature that you can find as liquids, as solids, and as liquid/solid combinations.

© Harcourt Achieve Inc. All rights reserved.

Name ______________________________ Date ______________

Experiment 3: Covered with Dirt

Purpose Being covered with dirt can change some solids. In this experiment, you will discover some things that can change and how they change.

Materials

adult helper

rectangle-shaped planter (approx. 2 feet x 8 inches) full of dirt

2 galvanized bolts

1 piece of watermelon (about 2 inches W x 2 inches L x $\frac{1}{4}$ inch deep) without rind

1 piece of watermelon rind (about 2 inches L x $\frac{1}{2}$ inch W)

4 watermelon seeds

water in watering can

4 tongue depressors

fine black marker

Procedure

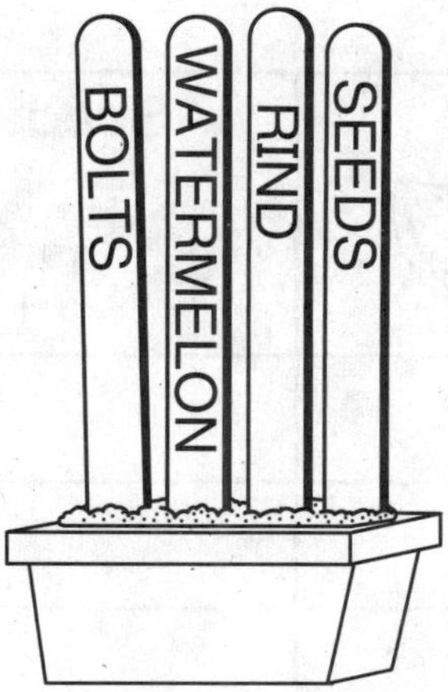

1. Use the black marker to write one of these words on each of the four tongue depressors: bolts, watermelon, rind, seeds.
2. Dig four 3-inch-deep holes spaced across the planter.
3. Plant the bolts in one hole, the watermelon rind in one hole, the watermelon seeds in one hole, and the watermelon in one hole.
4. Cover all the holes with dirt.
5. Place the correct tongue depressor next to each covered item so you can remember what is planted in each place.
6. Place the planter in sunlight. Watch the planter for 6 weeks.
7. Add about 2 cups of water each week. Spread the water over the whole planter.
8. Fill in the Results Table at the end of every two weeks.
9. After six weeks, dig up the solids you planted. Fill in the Results Table.

© Harcourt Achieve Inc. All rights reserved.

Name ______________________ Date ____________

Results

Use these numbers for your responses:

1 (no change)
2 (something is growing)
3 (the solid under the dirt is starting to fall apart)
4 (the solid under the dirt has fallen completely apart)
5 (cannot find anything under the dirt)

Describe what you see . . .	**Bolts** 	**Watermelon** 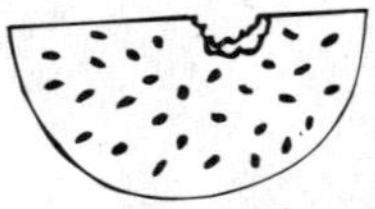	**Rind** 	**Seeds** 
2 weeks				
4 weeks				
6 weeks				
When you dig it up				

Conclusions

Read each statement. Circle the correct answer.

1. Choose the one that is supported by your results.
   A. Metal falls apart quickly under dirt.
   B. Seeds fall apart quickly under dirt.
   C. Soft foods fall apart quickly under dirt.
2. Choose the one that is supported by your results.
   A. Some plant parts last longer under dirt than others do.
   B. Seeds do not change under dirt.
   C. If left under dirt for 10 weeks, bolts would probably change.

© Harcourt Achieve Inc. All rights reserved.

Name ______________________ Date ____________

Lesson 3: Background

Look up! Where did you look? How did you know where to look?

A word like <u>up</u> can only be used when you **compare** at least two things. When you look up in the classroom, you are comparing where you are to where the ceiling is.

Is up always over your head? Think about if you were standing on your hands. Where would up be then?

You can also use other types of describing words to compare things. For example, one thing might be heavier than another or stickier than another.

Without something to compare it to, you cannot describe where a thing is. For example, if you are told the markers are "over there," do you know just where they are? If you are told that the markers are "under the window," do you know where they are?

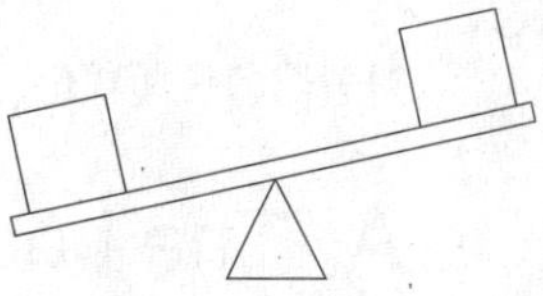

You can also use the way things relate to each other to describe how to **balance** them. You can move things closer or farther away. You can put something to the side or in the center.

Connection to Life Science

Have you ever stood on one leg? Try it now. Do you wobble?

As a rule, nothing that is bigger (like the top of a human body) balances very well on anything that is smaller (like one leg).

Now stand with your legs spaced apart. Do you wobble now? Even though human legs are not big, when you space them apart you get balance to your body.

© Harcourt Achieve Inc. All rights reserved.

Name ______________________________ Date ______________

Experiment 1: Bigger Than the Thing Behind It

Materials
room with a door
a book
some other object

Purpose Whether something is large or small depends on what you compare it to. Words like <u>left</u> and <u>right</u> can only be used when at least two things are compared. In this experiment, you will use one thing to describe another thing.

Procedure

1. Look around the room and find the objects in bold below.
2. Complete the statements about each object.

Results

1. Look at the **door** to the room. Use the background to describe the door.

   A. The door is to the left of ____________________.

   B. The door is to the right of ____________________.

2. Find a **book** in the room. Describe the book in relation to other things around it.

   A. The book is bigger than a ____________________ that is near it.

   B. The book is smaller than a ____________________ that is near it.

   C. The book is (under, above) a ____________________ that is near it.

3. Choose **another object** in the classroom. Describe the object in relation to its background.

   A. The (name of object) ____________________ is bigger than a ____________________ that is near it.

© Harcourt Achieve Inc. All rights reserved.

Name ______________________________ Date ______________

B. The (name of object) ______________ is smaller than a ______________ that is near it.

C. The (name of object) ______________ is (under, above) a ______________ that is near it.

Conclusions

Circle the correct answer.

1. One thing you can tell about the door by looking at things around it is—

A. where the door is located.

B. the color of the door.

C. what the door is made of.

2. One thing you can say about the book by looking at things around it is—

A. the title.

B. how much the book weighs.

C. if the book is big or small.

3. By looking at the things around the book, you can tell—

A. how many pages it has.

B. if it is in a high or low spot in the room.

C. how much the book costs.

Connection to Life Science

What are three things you can learn about a plant by looking at what is around it? Make a list. Then show your list in a drawing.

© Harcourt Achieve Inc. All rights reserved.

Name ______________________ Date ______________

Experiment 2: Pencil Balance

Purpose You can balance a pencil on a cup. You can identify the center point of both the pencil and the cup. You can also tell where the pencil is placed by comparing the locations of the center points.

Materials

adult helper

polystyrene cup (coffee cup)

new, sharpened pencil

pen

2 eraser caps

six $1\frac{3}{4}$-inch paper clips

$6\frac{1}{2}$ inch x $\frac{3}{8}$ inch strip of masking tape

Procedure

1. Place the tape under the pencil drawing on page 25. Have an adult use the pen to help you copy the grid that is on the pencil drawing onto the masking tape.
2. Center your pencil on the edge of the pencil grid on page 25 so you can see the numbers, letters, and lines. You can know your pencil is centered when the number of extra numbers on the left and the number of extra letters on the right are equal. Write an X to mark the center of the pencil.
3. Remove the masking tape from your paper and stick it on your pencil. Line up the center of the pencil with the center mark on the tape. If the tape strip is longer than your pencil, tear off the extra on each end.
4. Have an adult help you draw a line to mark the center of the cup bottom.
5. Match the center of the pencil with the center X on the cup so the pencil balances on top of the cup. Note in the Results Table that the X is entered as the starting point where the pencil lines up to the cup.
6. Add one eraser on the eraser end of the pencil. Move the pencil as needed so that it can balance on the cup. Write the correct number or letter of the mark that lines up with the center point on the cup in the Results Table.

© Harcourt Achieve Inc. All rights reserved.

Name ______________________________ Date ________________

7. Add a second eraser by pushing it onto the end of the first eraser. Balance the pencil and write the letter or number in the Results Table.

8. Remove the erasers.

9. Place six paper clips on the sharpened end of the pencil. Balance the pencil and write the correct letter or number in the Results Table.

10. Balance the pencil with one eraser and six paper clips. Write the correct letter or number in the Results Table.

11. Balance the pencil with two erasers and six paper clips. Write the correct letter or number in the Results Table.

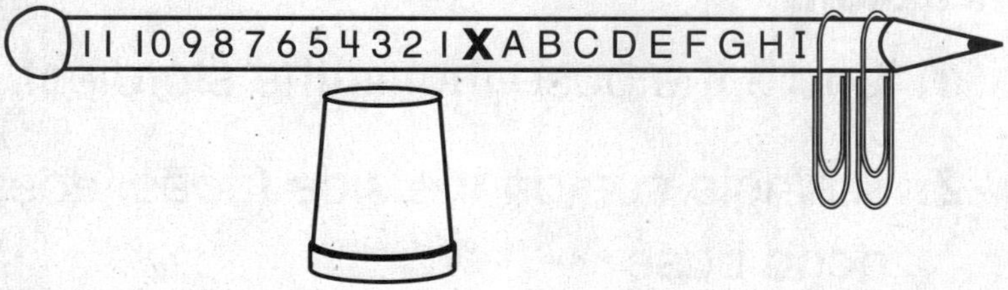

Results

	Point on pencil that matches middle of cup
Starting point (pencil only)	X
With 1 eraser	
With 2 erasers	
With 6 paper clips	
With 2 erasers and 6 paper clips	

Conclusions

Circle the correct word or words that best complete each sentence.

1. With no erasers or paper clips on it, the pencil balances on the cup as long as the two (centers, ends) are lined up.

2. When the pencil is balanced with two erasers on it, the center of the cup is closer to the (eraser end, sharpened end) of the pencil.

© Harcourt Achieve Inc. All rights reserved.

Name ______________________________ Date ______________

Experiment 3: Tower Balance

Purpose A tower can be very high if it is built with balance. In this experiment, you will use **trial and error** to build a balanced tower.

Materials

twenty 8-ounce paper cups

8 cardboard sheets, each about $8\frac{1}{2}$ inches x 11 inches

Procedure

1. Use the cups and cardboards to build the towers that are shown.
2. After working with each tower, circle the word or words that best complete the results statements and answer the questions.

Results and Conclusions

Tower Bases
(Try all three.)

Tower #1

Tower #2

1. Circle the base that is the sturdiest.
2. A single cup on the side (does, does not) make a good base.
3. A single cup in the middle (does, does not) make a good base.
4. Four spread-out cups (do, do not) make a good base.
5. Circle all the levels that are balanced in Tower #1: bottom, 2nd, 3rd, top
6. With a good base, the balance of each level (is still important, will not matter).
7. Is Tower #2 steady? Tell why. ______________________________

   ____

8. It is easier to build a tall tower when (there are only four levels, all the levels are balanced).

© Harcourt Achieve Inc. All rights reserved.

Name ______________________________ Date ______________

Tower #3

9. Which of the levels in Tower #3 are well-balanced?

____

10. Does the tower stand up even though not all the levels are well-balanced? ______________________

11. If the base is balanced, you might be able to build a tower with some upper levels that are not as (high, balanced).

Plan a tower that uses all the cups and cardboards. Make the tower as high as you can make it. Draw a picture of your plan. Then build the tower.

12. Were you able to make your tower stand up? ______________________

13. Did you make any changes from your plan? ______________________

If so, why? ______________________

Connection to Earth Science

Find a picture of a mountain. Tell how this experiment relates to a mountain.

© Harcourt Achieve Inc. All rights reserved.

Name ______________________________ Date ______________

Lesson 4: Background

Have you ever seen a book slide itself across the floor of a room?

Have you ever seen a glass cup move across a table on its own?

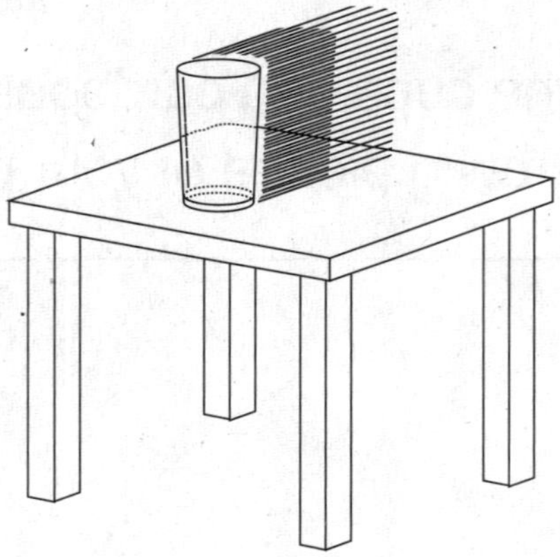

Of course you have not seen a book or a glass move on its own! Objects that are **nonliving** do not move without help. How far an object moves depends on two things:

- how much **force** pushed or pulled on it
- the **weight** of the object

Objects like a wagon on a hill, a swing in the wind, and a motorcycle going down a street cannot move on their own. These objects require a push or a pull.

Connection to Life Science

Animals are alive and can move on their own. Plants are alive, but cannot move on their own. But sometimes plants can move in other ways. Find five things that could cause plants to move.

© Harcourt Achieve Inc. All rights reserved.

Name ______________________ Date ____________

Experiment 1: Moving a Little and a Lot

Purpose Objects move differently based on how hard they are pushed. You will measure movements based on three different kinds of "pushes."

Materials

8-ounce plastic cup	10 sheets of paper
cellophane tape	marker

Procedure

1. Tape 10 sheets of paper together, end to end.
2. Write the numbers 1–10 on the papers.

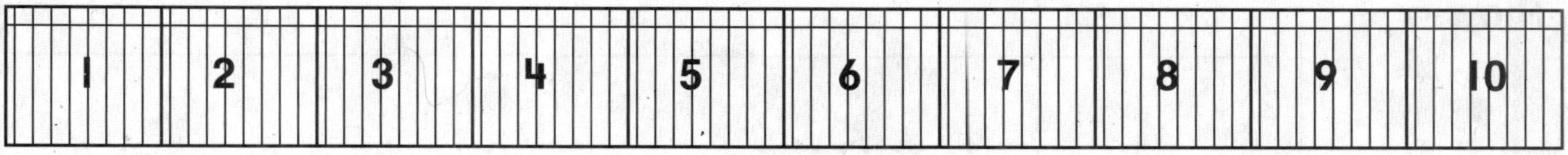

3. Place the strip of papers on the floor in an open area.
4. Place the plastic cup at the edge of the #1 sheet of paper.
5. Lie down on your stomach with your head facing the cup and blow as hard as you can. See how far down the line of papers you can blow the cup.
6. Record the distance in the Results Table by writing down the number of the paper it lands on.
7. Try blowing the cup one more time from the starting point and record your results.

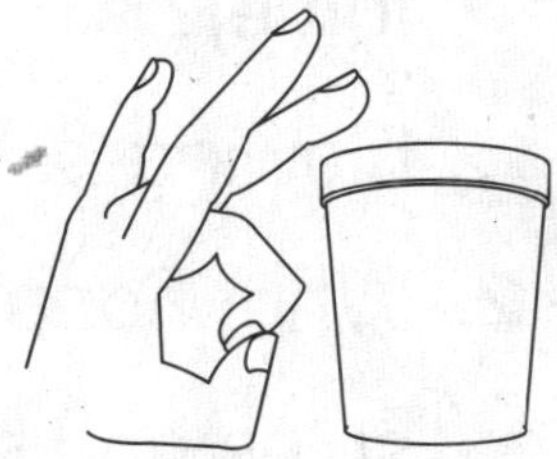

8. Place the cup back at the starting point.
9. Using your thumb and middle finger, flick the cup.
10. Record the number where the cup lands.
11. Repeat the flicking from the starting point one more time.
12. Record your results.

© Harcourt Achieve Inc. All rights reserved.

Name ______________________________ Date ______________

13. Place the cup back at the starting point.

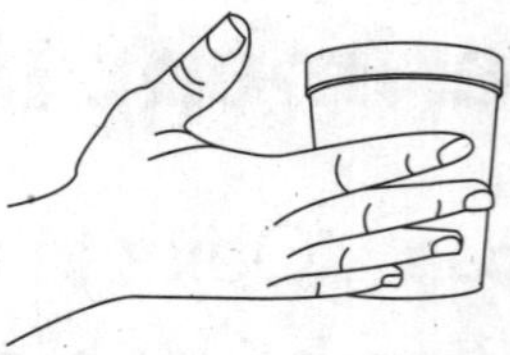

14. Hit it with your open hand.

15. Record the page number where it lands. If it lands past the last sheet of paper, write Past 10.

16. Repeat the open hand hit from the starting point one more time.

17. Record your results.

Results

Action	Trial #	Number where stopped
Blowing	1	
	2	
Flicking	1	
	2	
Hitting	1	
	2	

Conclusions

Circle the correct answer.

1. Which of the three caused the cup to move the farthest (had more force)?

   blowing   flicking   hitting

2. What happens when the cup is hit with more force?

   spins and stops   moves farther and faster   breaks

Connection to Earth Science

Think about storms that blow a little, a little more, and a lot. Explain how a toy wagon in the front yard might react to each type of storm.

© Harcourt Achieve Inc. All rights reserved.

Name ______________________ Date ____________

Experiment 2: Weight Matters

Purpose Different sizes and weights of objects affect the amount of force needed to move the objects. You will explore what it takes to move different objects.

Materials

- 10 sheets of paper
- cellophane tape
- marker
- 0.5 L water bottle, full
- 0.5 L water bottle, $\frac{3}{4}$ full
- 0.5 L water bottle, half full
- 0.5 L water bottle, $\frac{1}{4}$ full
- 0.5 L water bottle, empty

Procedure

1. Tape 10 sheets of paper together, end to end.
2. Write the numbers 1–10 on the papers.

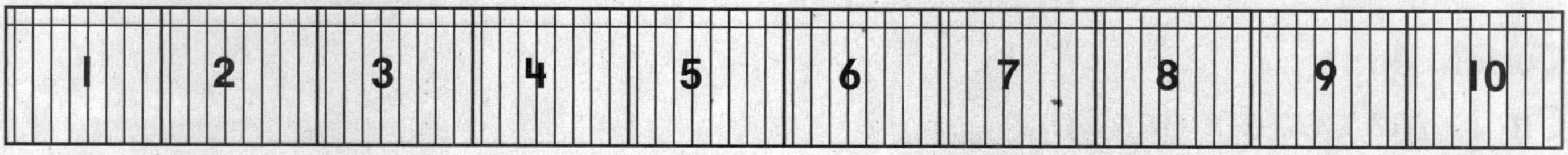

3. Place the strip of papers on the floor in an open area.
4. Place the empty water bottle at the edge of the #1 piece of paper. See how far down the line of papers you can blow the bottle.
5. Record the distance in the Results Table by noting the number of the paper it landed on.
6. Return the empty bottle to the starting point.
7. Using your thumb and middle finger, flick the bottle.
8. Record the number where the bottle stops.
9. Return the empty bottle to the starting point.
10. Raise your arm up to shoulder height. Then, using your open hand, hit the bottle.
11. Record the number of the paper where the bottle lands.
12. Repeat Steps 4–11 with each of the other four bottles.

© Harcourt Achieve Inc. All rights reserved.

Name ______________________________ Date ______________

Results

Water levels	Blowing	Flicking	Hitting
empty			
$\frac{1}{4}$ full			
$\frac{1}{2}$ full			
$\frac{3}{4}$ full			
full			

Conclusions

Circle the correct answer.

1. Even a little bit of weight is too much when trying to move the bottle by—

   A. blowing. **B.** flicking. **C.** hitting.

2. All the different weighted bottles can be moved by—

   A. blowing. **B.** flicking. **C.** hitting.

3. One thing that you probably could not move by blowing, flicking, or hitting is a—

   A. 3-foot-tall concrete pillar.

   B. 5-foot-tall beach ball.

Connection to Life Science

Think about how this experiment relates to dandelions that have turned white and fuzzy. Why are the seeds easily blown around? Do you think the new seeds are usually planted next to the old plant? Learn more about this and tell why.

© Harcourt Achieve Inc. All rights reserved.

Name ______________________________ Date ______________

Experiment 3: It's All in How You Hit It!

Purpose The amount of swing and whether or not you follow through both make a big difference in how far you can hit a ball. In this experiment, you will explore the difference that swings and follow-throughs make.

Materials

adult helper to oversee students while outside

softball bat

eight softballs

softball base

for each student: 8 marker flags made out of tongue depressors and paper triangles with child's name and description of the swing type

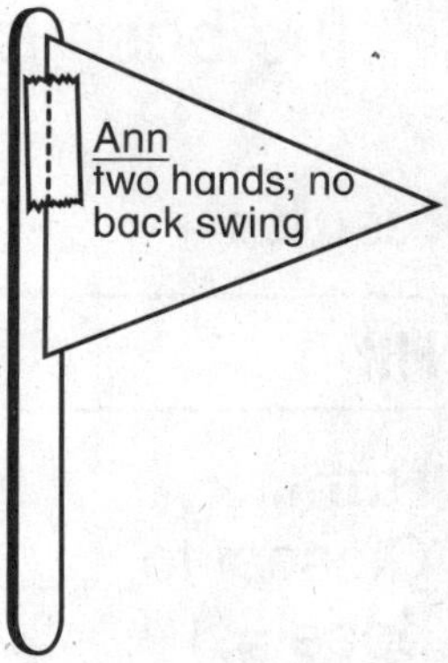

Procedure

1. Go to a baseball field or an open grassy area that could be used for a baseball field.
2. Place the base at home plate.
3. Take turns hitting balls with a bat, placing markers for the hits, and picking up the balls until all children have hit.
4. When it is your turn to hit, stand beside the base and, one at a time, place the balls on the base. Hit along the ground eight times as listed below and on the next page. Each time, hit as hard as possible. After each hit, have a partner place the correct marker where the ball stops.

Hit #	Hold bat in . . .	Hit the ball with . . .	Use a follow-through?
1	one hand	no back swing	no
2	one hand	waist-high back swing	no
3	one hand	shoulder-high back swing	no
4	one hand	shoulder-high back swing	yes, shoulder high
5	two hands	no back swing	no

© Harcourt Achieve Inc. All rights reserved.

Name ______________________________ Date ______________

Hit #	Hold bat in . . .	Hit the ball with . . .	Use a follow-through?
6	two hands	waist-high back swing	no
7	two hands	shoulder-high back swing	no
8	two hands	shoulder-high back swing	yes, shoulder high

5. Complete the Results Table. Rank the marker flags from closest to the base to farthest from the base.

Results

Hit	1	2	3	4	5	6	7	8
Rank Closest to base = 1 Farthest from base = 8								

Conclusions

Write how you would hold the bat and swing if you wanted to hit the ball in each of the following ways.

1. Just a few feet

____

2. To the pitcher on the pitcher's mound

____

Connection to Life Science

Think about standing near an elephant who is swinging his or her trunk. Why would you want to stand far away if the elephant took a big back swing? How does an elephant's trunk relate to this experiment?

© Harcourt Achieve Inc. All rights reserved.

Name ______________________________ Date ______________

Lesson 5: Background

Most **living things**, like animals and plants, look like their parents. In fact, they sometimes look so much like their parents that you can see just a part of a baby plant or animal and still match it to its parent.

For example, if you know that this is an elephant, you probably also recognize a baby elephant just by seeing this trunk.

If you have seen a black and white cow, you can probably recognize a calf by seeing only a part of its back.

If you know this is an onion, you can probably recognize growing onion plants.

If you see these two trees, you can probably figure out which one is the parent to this new baby tree.

Connection to Earth Science

Begin with four buckets of dirt from four different locations. Label the buckets 1–4. Using four small paper cups, take a sample from each bucket and write matching labels on the paper cups. Then, move the bucket labels to the bottoms of the buckets so they do not show. Switch the buckets around. Try to match the soil samples to the correct original buckets. Check your success.

© Harcourt Achieve Inc. All rights reserved.

Name ______________________ Date ____________

Experiment 1: Matching Leaves

Materials

full-grown leaf from each of 6 different types of trees or bushes

new small leaf from each of 6 very small trees or bushes or newly unfurled small leaves from grown trees or bushes (Small leaves should have a one-to-one match in type of tree or bush with the full-grown leaves.)

6 index cards numbered 1–6

Purpose Plants and animals look like their parents. In this experiment, you will match new young leaves to full-sized leaves of the same type.

Procedure

1. Place the full-sized leaves in one row.

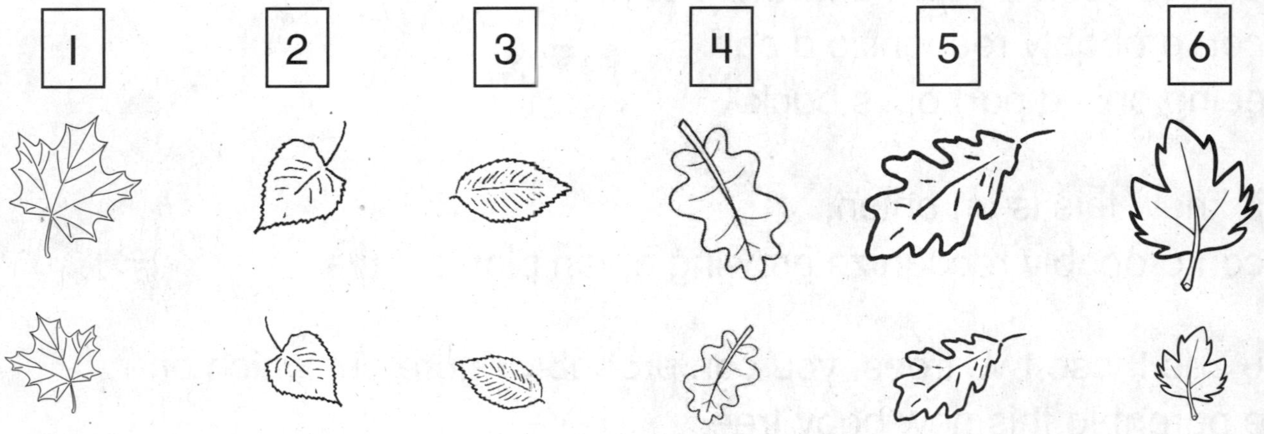

2. Place the index cards in order above the leaves.
3. Match the new, small leaves to the full-grown leaves of the same type of tree or bush.
4. Place the small leaves under the matching full-sized leaves.

Results

Write yes or no to answer each question.

1. Was it easy to tell which leaves were the full-grown leaves?

   ____

2. Did you find one young leaf to match each full-grown leaf?

   ____

© Harcourt Achieve Inc. All rights reserved.

Name ______________________ Date ____________

3. Ask a friend to look at your matches. Does he or she agree that your matches are correct? ______________

Conclusions

Complete this table to tell how the large and small leaves are alike and different.

	How are the leaves alike?	How are the leaves different?
#1		
#2		
#3		
#4		
#5		
#6		

Circle the word or words that best complete the sentence.

The leaves from these six types of trees or bushes show that young plants (do, do not) look a lot like their parents.

Connection to Earth Science

Study some topsoil from a wooded area. Sort out pieces of leaves that you can see. Scientists study rocks that are thousands of years old. Why do you think it is very strange to study leaves that are that old?

© Harcourt Achieve Inc. All rights reserved.

Name ______________________ Date ______________

Experiment 2: Growing Mixed Plants

Materials

large planter, about 2 feet x 1 foot filled with dirt

3 mixed seeds, such as radish, lettuce, and zinnia

water in watering container

pictures of the 3 full-grown plants that are included in the seed mix

Purpose When new plants grow out of the ground, you can usually tell what kind of plants they are since they look like their parent plants. You will plant some mixed seeds and then identify them.

Procedure

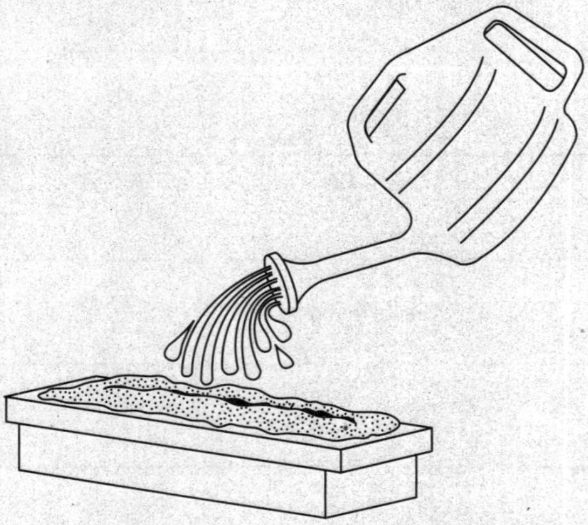

1. Dig a trench down the center of the planter.
2. Pour about 1 cup of water along the trench.
3. Plant a handful of mixed seeds in the trench.
4. Cover the seeds with dirt.
5. Add 1 cup of water to the planter every day for four weeks or until three different kinds of plants grow out of the soil.
6. Compare the baby plants to the plant pictures and try to identify them.

© Harcourt Achieve Inc. All rights reserved.

Name ____________________ Date ____________

Results

Answer the questions.

1. How long after you planted the seeds did the first plants grow through the dirt? ____________________

2. In what ways do the baby plants look like the grown plants?

____

3. How many of each small plant have grown?

(Name of plant) ____________ How many? ________

(Name of plant) ____________ How many? ________

(Name of plant) ____________ How many? ________

Conclusions

Circle the word that best completes each sentence.

1. As soon as you see the first tip of green growing, you (can, cannot) identify the baby plants.
2. After they have been up for one week, you (can, cannot) identify the baby plants.

Connection to Earth Science

Study some hard dirt and some soft dirt. Why do you think new young plants almost never grow in dirt that is really hard?

© Harcourt Achieve Inc. All rights reserved.

Name ______________________ Date ______________

Experiment 3: Growing Apple Tree Leaves

Purpose The fruit from a tree has seeds that can grow a new tree. In this experiment, you will show that an apple seed does grow into an apple tree.

Materials

adult helper

apple with a leaf still attached or a loose leaf from the apple tree

knife

large planter, about 2 feet x 1 foot filled with dirt

water in a watering container

small plastic zipper bag

heavy book

Procedure

1. Have an adult use the knife to help cut the apple open.
2. Remove the seeds.
3. Dig three holes (about 3 inches deep) spaced across the planter.
4. Place three apple seeds in each hole.
5. Pour about 1 cup of water in each hole.
6. Cover the seeds with dirt.
7. Place the apple tree leaf in the plastic bag.
8. Place the bag inside a large book so that the leaf is pressed flat.

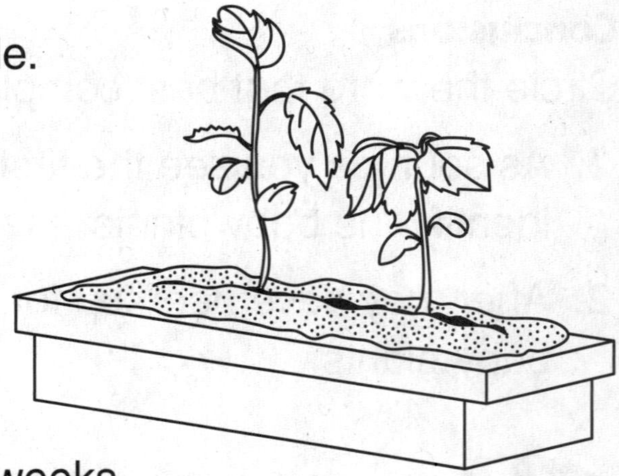

9. Watch the apple seeds grow for four weeks.
10. Record what you see in the table on the next page.
11. Every three days, pour 1 cup of water on each seed area.
12. When the new plants are big enough that you can look at the leaves, compare new leaves to the pressed leaf.
13. Record what you see in the Results Table.

Note: If you cannot find an apple leaf, use a picture of an apple leaf instead and do not do steps 7 and 8. For step 12, compare the leaves to the picture.

© Harcourt Achieve Inc. All rights reserved.

Name ______________________ Date ____________

Results

	What you see . . .
Week One	
Week Two	
Week Three	
Week Four	
New Leaves Compared to Pressed Leaf	

Conclusions

Circle the correct answer.

1. The leaves from apple, pear, and orange trees are probably—

   A. all bigger than lemon tree leaves.

   B. all just like peach tree leaves.

   C. all a little different from each other.

2. Many apple seeds—

   A. never get planted.

   B. are bigger than a marble.

   C. grow into oranges.

Connection to Physical Science

Apple trees grow more fruit some years. In a picture, show why the apple tree limbs are in danger of breaking during the good years.

© Harcourt Achieve Inc. All rights reserved.

Name ______________________ Date ______________

Lesson 6: Background

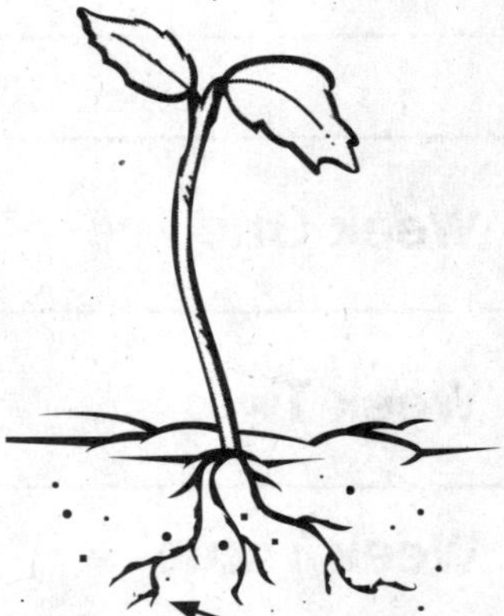

Plants, like people, have basic **needs**. Like you, plants need air, water, and light to survive in their **habitats**.

Plants get water.

When it rains, water goes into the **soil**. It might rain on a plant's leaves, but the plant leaves cannot drink the rainwater.

The plant's **roots** take the water from the soil. The water then goes up the plant's roots to its **stem**. From the stem, the water goes to the rest of the plant.

Plants that are cut and put in vases don't have roots. So the water goes into the stems in these plants.

Plants get light.

Plants get light from the **sun**. The light from the sun gives them **energy**. In a place like a **cave** and a **forest**, there is not much light. So many plants will not grow there.

Plants use the light to grow and make their own food. A big word for the way plants make their own food is **photosynthesis**.

Plants get air.

Plants get air through openings on the bottom sides of their leaves. These openings are called **stomata**. The openings are so small that you cannot see them without a **microscope**.

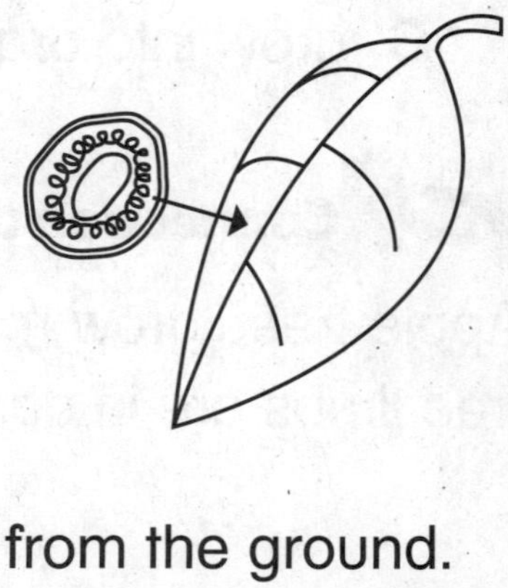

Connection to Earth Science

When plants die, they turn into soil. Fill a pail with soil from the ground. Sort through the pail and see if you can find any plant parts in it.

© Harcourt Achieve Inc. All rights reserved.

Name ____________________ Date ____________

Experiment 1: Coloring Flowers

Purpose Water goes up plant stems to its leaves and flowers. In this experiment, you will use colored water so you can see where the water goes.

Materials
- adult helper
- 4 white carnations with about 8-inch stems
- 4 glasses $\frac{3}{4}$ full of water
- blue, green, and red food coloring
- blue, green, and red markers
- scissors

Procedure

1. Add 20 drops of red food coloring to one glass of water.
2. Add 20 drops of blue food coloring to another glass of water.
3. Add 20 drops of green food coloring to the third glass of water.
4. Do not add anything to the last glass of water.
5. Have an adult helper use the scissors to trim about 1 inch off of each flower stem.
6. Place a carnation in each glass.
7. Watch for color changes in the carnations.
8. Every 2 hours, record what you see in the Results Table.

Results

Use the markers to show how the carnations change. Color the parts of the flowers that show color.

Colors	2 hours	4 hours	6 hours
Red			
Green			

© Harcourt Achieve Inc. All rights reserved.

Name ______________________ Date ____________

Colors	2 hours	4 hours	6 hours
Blue			
Plain			

Conclusions

Circle the correct answer.

1. How can you tell the water went up the stems?
   - **A.** The stems turned the colors of the water.
   - **B.** The stems are wet so water had to go through them.
   - **C.** The water had to go through the stems to get to the flowers.
2. How fast do flowers drink water?
   - **A.** Slower than people do
   - **B.** The same as people do
   - **C.** Faster than people do

Answer the question.

3. How does the flower in plain water show that the food coloring causes the color changes?

____

____

Connection to Earth Science

Find pictures of at least three different-colored wildflowers. Do you think these flowers get their color from the color of water? Tell why.

© Harcourt Achieve Inc. All rights reserved.

Name ______________________ Date ______________

Experiment 2: A Fight for Light

Materials

adult helper	three standard large-sized tissue boxes
two 4 x 6 index cards	duct tape or packaging tape
scissors	plant pot that is full of soil and will fit in the shoe box
watering can with water	bean seed that has been soaked in water for at least 24 hours

Purpose Plants need light and they will grow towards it. In this experiment, you will grow a plant that bends and twists to reach the light.

Procedure

1. Stack the two index cards and tape them over half of the opening of one of the tissue boxes. Also, cut out the bottom.

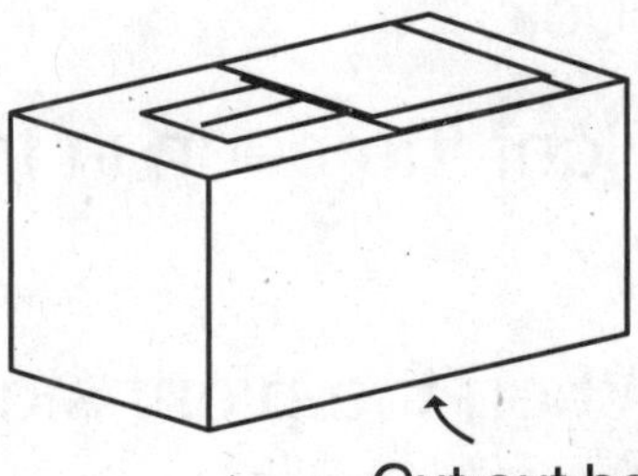

2. On the top, make the opening beside the index cards bigger. Cut along the sides of the index cards and to all three edges of the box.

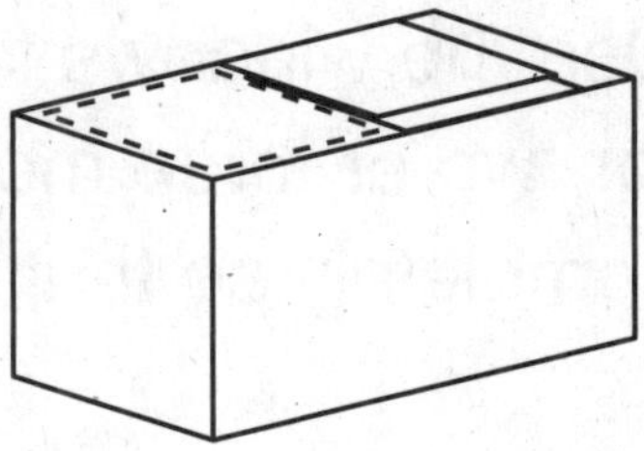

3. Cut the same size larger opening in each of the other two tissue boxes. Then, as shown, cut two doors in one of the boxes and one in the other. Cut on the edges and fold on the dotted lines to create doors as shown. Place tape on the side of the box and on each door so you can easily open and close the doors.

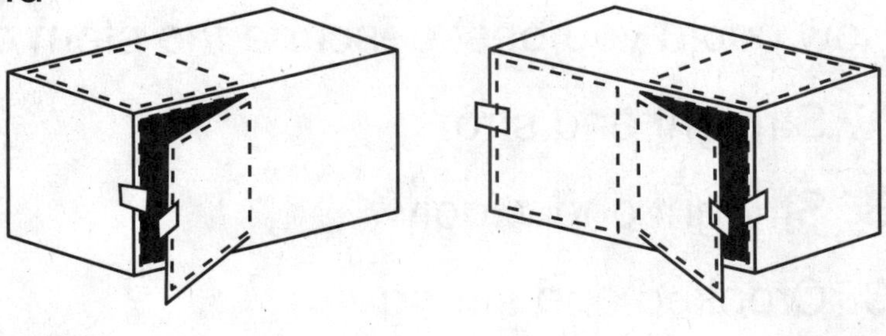

© Harcourt Achieve Inc. All rights reserved.

Name ______________________________ Date ______________

4. In each of the boxes without the index cards, cut the same size opening in the bottom of the box on the opposite end.

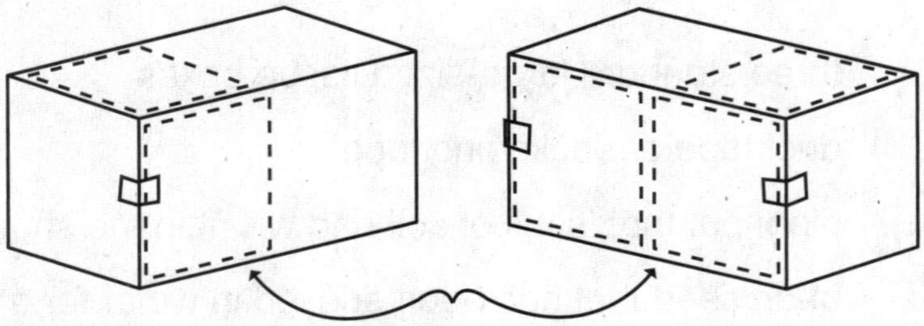

5. Stack the boxes as shown.
6. Tape the boxes together on the sides and back.
7. Plant the bean in the plant pot and water it.
8. When the plant starts to grow, place it in the bottom box through the open bottom.
9. Use the door above the plant pot to water the plant every three days.
10. Use the windows to watch the plant grow for two or three months. Make sure to always close the doors completely so that the light does not go in through the doors.

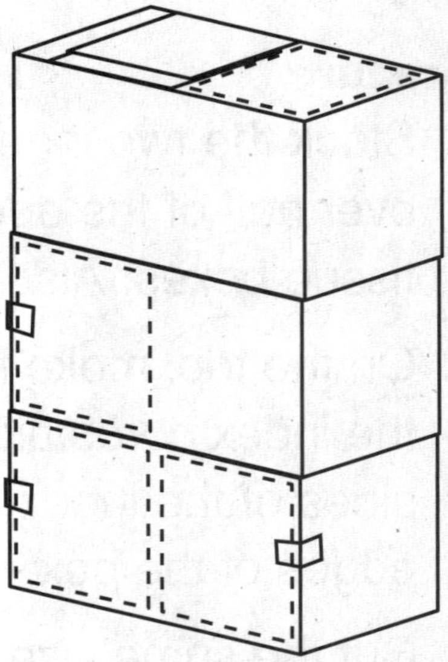

Results

Answer these questions after the plant shows in the hole at the top of the stack of boxes. Circle the correct answer.

1. How could you best describe the stem of this plant?

   A. Straight and strong

   B. Straight and wiggly

   C. Crooked and strong

© Harcourt Achieve Inc. All rights reserved.

Name ______________________ Date __________

2. How could you describe the directions the plant grew?

   A. It grew only sideways.

   B. It grew over and up towards the light.

   C. It grew only upwards.

Conclusions

Answer the questions.

1. How does this plant look different from a regular bean plant?

   ____

   ____

2. How did this plant show that it needed light?

   ____

   ____

3. What do you think would have happened to this plant if light could not go into the hole at the top of the stack?

   ____

   ____

Connection to Earth Science

Draw a picture showing a place in nature where plants cannot get enough light to grow.

© Harcourt Achieve Inc. All rights reserved.

Name ________________________________ Date ______________

Experiment 3: Air Control

Materials

healthy potted plant with at least 6 healthy leaves

petroleum jelly

paper towels

Purpose Plants need air to breathe. In this experiment, you will find out what happens when plant leaves cannot get air.

Procedure

1. Cover the tops of two healthy leaves with petroleum jelly.
2. Cover the bottoms of two healthy leaves with petroleum jelly.
3. Clean your hands with the paper towels.
4. Leave the plant alone for two days.
5. Complete the Results Table to show how the leaves compare after two days.

Results

	Leaf color	Leaf sturdiness
Leaves with petroleum jelly on the tops		
Leaves with petroleum jelly on the bottoms		
Leaves with no petroleum jelly		

Conclusions

Circle the correct answer.

This experiment shows that the leaves on this plant breathe from—

A. the top side.

B. the bottom side.

C. both the top and bottom sides.

Connection to Earth Science

Think about floods, volcanoes, and earthquakes. Draw a picture showing how nature might cut off a plant's air.

© Harcourt Achieve Inc. All rights reserved.

Name ______________________ Date ____________

Lesson 7: Background

All living things **react** to their **environment**, or the living and nonliving things around them. They do things to stay safe.

For example, you do some things because of how you feel.

- You sleep when you are tired.
- You eat when you are hungry.

You also use your **senses** for many things in life.

- You see an apple and eat it.
- You smell smoke and look to see what is burning.
- You feel something wet in your backpack and look to see what it is.
- You hear the phone ringing, so you answer it.
- You taste something bad, so you stop eating it.

Like people, insects also do some things because of their own needs.

- Insects walk and fly to move around.
- Insects find and eat food.

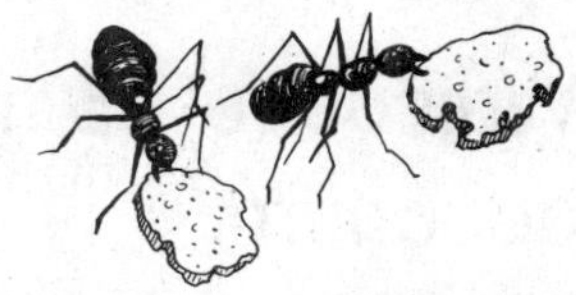

Also like people, insects do other things because of what they see, smell, touch, or hear.

- Some insects feel the air move if something gets near them, so they know to move.
- When it gets cold, some insects feel the heat in buildings and try to get inside them to stay warm.
- Some insects see the bright colors or smell the nice **scents** of flowers and go to them.

Connection to Physical Science

Choose a colorful plant that insects might fly to. Get ten 1-gram weights and add them one at a time to see how much weight the plant can hold before it bends over. Find out how much five different insects weigh.

© Harcourt Achieve Inc. All rights reserved.

Name ______________________ Date ______________

Experiment 1: Ladybug World

Purpose As a ladybug walks around, it naturally changes directions sometimes. It might also react to things in its way. In this experiment, you will explore how ladybugs move.

Materials

2 or more ladybugs

5–10 gallon aquarium with a lid

mixture of twigs, leaves, and small rocks

whistle

small, bright-beamed flashlight

medicine dropper filled with water

Procedure

1. Place twigs, leaves, and small rocks in the bottom of the aquarium.
2. Place the ladybugs in the aquarium.
3. Put the lid on.
4. Watch how the ladybugs move for about 2 minutes.
5. Record what you see in the Results Table. Circle yes or no in the last 2 columns.
6. Wait about 15 minutes to give the ladybugs time to get used to the aquarium.
7. Watch how the ladybugs move for another 2 minutes.
8. Record what you see in the Results Table.
9. Remove the lid.
10. Blow the whistle close to a ladybug.
11. Record what you see in the Results Table.
12. Shine the light on a ladybug.
13. Record what you see in the Results Table.
14. Drop a few drops of water on a ladybug.
15. Record what you see in the Results Table.
16. Put the lid back on.

© Harcourt Achieve Inc. All rights reserved.

Name ______________________________ Date ______________

Results

	What did the ladybugs do?	Natural move for ladybug?	Reaction to environment?
First 2-minute watch		yes no	yes no
Second 2-minute watch		yes no	yes no
Whistle		yes no	yes no
Light		yes no	yes no
Water		yes no	yes no

Conclusions

Circle the correct answer based on your results.

1. Ladybugs usually—
   A. walk over things in their way.
   B. walk around things in their way.
   C. dig under things in their way.
2. If it is raining, ladybugs will probably—
   A. walk but not take cover.
   B. try to get under something.
   C. sit in the rain and get wet.
3. When they hear a loud sound, ladybugs will probably—
   A. run quickly.
   B. hide under something.
   C. make no change in what they are doing.

Connection to Earth Science

Have you ever seen a ladybug crawling on a snowbank? Search the Internet to find out if ladybugs crawl around in snow.

© Harcourt Achieve Inc. All rights reserved.

Name ______________________________ Date ______________

Experiment 2: Mealworm Run

Materials

adult helper

for every 3 children: mealworm; 2 feet of string; ruler; approximately 12 inch x 12 inch piece of sandpaper, fabric, wax paper covered with sugar or flour, paper, plastic wrap, plywood, tinfoil

black marker

Purpose People find it easier to run on some surfaces. In this experiment, you will see how mealworms react to different surfaces.

Procedure

Place a black dot at about the center of each surface. Then follow these steps for each surface:

1. Place the mealworm on the dot and start timing.
2. Let the mealworm move around for 2 minutes.
3. Each time the mealworm turns a new direction, make a dot at the turn point.

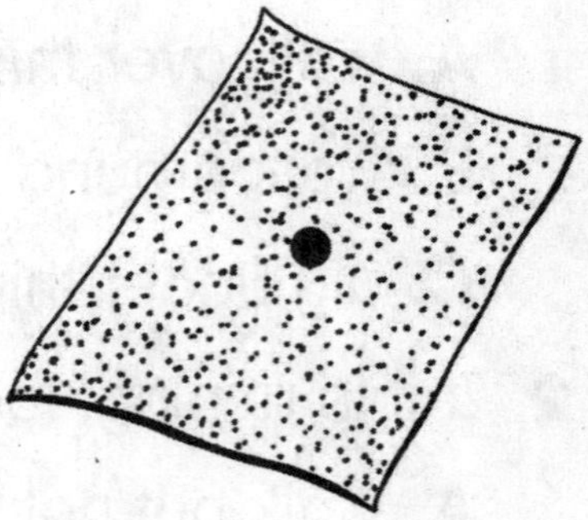

4. At the end of 2 minutes, make a dot where the mealworm stops.
5. Connect the dots.
6. Lay the string around the connected path.
7. Use your finger and thumb to mark the string at the end of the part that you used to line the path.
8. Lay the string in an L shape, bending at the point where you stopped using the string.
9. Use the ruler to measure the string that you used.
10. Write this number in the Results Table. This is the distance the mealworm moved.

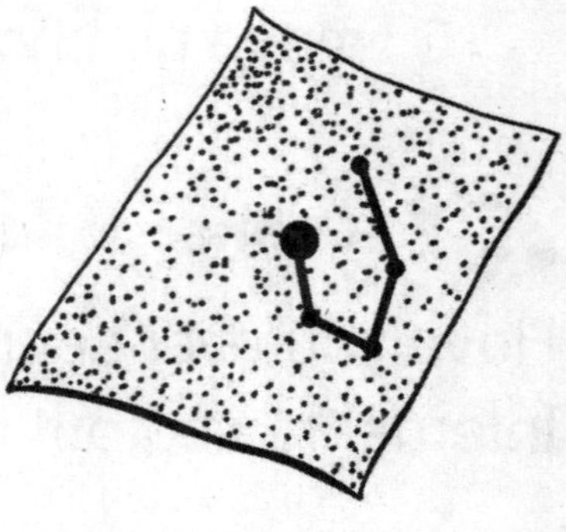

© Harcourt Achieve Inc. All rights reserved.

Name ______________________ Date ______________

Results

Surface	Distance moved	Rank (1 = most distance; 7 = least distance)
Sandpaper		
Fabric		
Sugar or flour		
Paper		
Plastic wrap		
Plywood		
Tinfoil		

Conclusions

Complete each sentence.

1. My mealworm moved the most on ______________.
2. My mealworm moved the least on ______________.

Circle the correct answer.

3. Based on our results, it seems that mealworms—
   A. do not care what they walk on.
   B. only have one or two surfaces they do not like.
   C. only have one or two surfaces they do like.

Connection to Earth Science

In this experiment, you worked with different man-made surfaces. Many different surfaces also exist naturally. Identify at least five different surfaces that exist naturally.

© Harcourt Achieve Inc. All rights reserved.

Name ________________________________ Date ______________

Experiment 3: Smelling Who It Is

Materials

adult helper

small zipper bag for each child

paper towel for each child

for each 2 children, one of the following: banana, bar soap, black licorice, butterscotch, ketchup, cinnamon, coffee, garlic, grapefruit, horseradish, lemon, mustard, onion, peanut butter, peppermint, rubbing alcohol, vanilla, vinegar

Purpose Many insects use smells to communicate. They may know each other only by smell. In this experiment, you will practice communicating by smell.

Procedure

Prepare the scent bags with the help of an adult.

1. Pour or rub a small amount of each scent on two paper towels and fold the towels.
2. Place each paper towel in a plastic bag and seal the bag.
3. Mix the bags up so the pairs are not together.

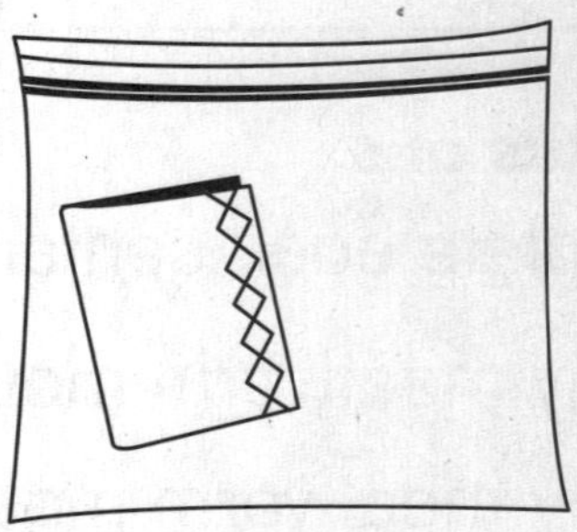

Use the scent bags.

4. Take one scent bag.
5. Without talking, find the person who has the same scent.
6. Make sure not to put the scent bag close to your nose.

Results

Answer the questions.

1. What scent do you have? Circle your answer.

banana butterscotch coffee horseradish onion rubbing alcohol

bar soap ketchup garlic lemon peanut butter vanilla

black licorice cinnamon grapefruit mustard peppermint vinegar

2. Who has the same scent as you have? ______________________

3. How did you find the person with the same scent? ______________

____

© Harcourt Achieve Inc. All rights reserved.

Name ______________________ Date ____________

Conclusions

Answer the question.

1. Think about recognizing your friends every day by smell instead of by sight. Do you think it would be a harder way to recognize your friends?

   Tell why. ______________________

   ____

Circle the correct answer.

2. What would make this experiment hard to do?

   A. not knowing someone's name

   B. not being able to hear

   C. having a cold

3. You might not have thought about it, but you probably already know your friends by—

   A. hearing.

   B. touching.

   C. smelling.

Connection to Physical Science

The scents of some materials are easier to tell when wet. For example, compare the smells of these things wet and dry: peppermint and bubble gum. The scents of some materials are also more noticeable when heated. For example, compare the smells of these things at room temperature and heated: meat and bread.

© Harcourt Achieve Inc. All rights reserved.

Name ______________________________ Date ______________

Lesson 8: Background

Plants and animals **inherit** things that make them look and act like their parents. For example, children can inherit the color of their hair from their parents.

Animals inherit the ability to hide in their environment. When a plant or animal hides by blending into its environment, it is known as **camouflage**.

Animals also inherit the ability to find food. They find food when they are hungry.

Animals are born knowing how to do many things. Even though they are born to do most things they need to do, animals also react to the world around them. When animals sense danger, they run away.

Connection to Physical Science

Ants can carry many times their own body weight. What about you? Can you carry more than your body weight? See how much weight you can easily carry. Weigh an empty bucket. Then fill it with water and weigh it. Use the bucket to fill a 5-gallon bucket so you can keep track of how much the large bucket weighs. Fill a second 5-gallon bucket. See if you can lift two small buckets, one large bucket, and two large buckets. To make sure you do not hurt yourself, do not try to lift something that feels too heavy. Are you like an ant? Can you lift two or three times your weight?

© Harcourt Achieve Inc. All rights reserved.

Name ______________________ Date ____________

Experiment 1: Hiding Insects

Purpose Many animals use camouflage to hide. In this experiment, you will design and look for camouflaged insects.

Materials	adult helper	bugs on this page	markers	pair of scissors	pencil

Procedure

1. Choose one of the four bugs and cut it out.
2. Find a spot to hide your bug in the room.
3. Color your bug with markers so it can hide in the spot you have picked.
4. On the back of your bug, describe the spot where the bug will hide.
5. Give your bug to your adult helper to place in your hiding spot when the room is empty.
6. After the bugs are all placed, go on a bug hunt.

Results

Answer the questions.

1. How many bugs were placed around the room? ______________
2. How many bugs did you find during the hunt? ______________

Conclusions

Answer the questions.

1. What is one thing that made a bug hard to find? ______________

____

2. What is one thing that made a bug easy to find? ______________

____

© Harcourt Achieve Inc. All rights reserved.

Name ______________________________ Date ____________

Experiment 2: Counting Legs and Body Parts

Purpose Bugs inherit the way they look from their parents. In this experiment, you will find bugs and compare them to pictures of different types of bugs.

Materials

adult helper

2 or 3 bugs per child (place them in a plastic bottle with air holes)

Procedure

1. Compare your bugs to the pictures below.
2. Complete the Results Table.

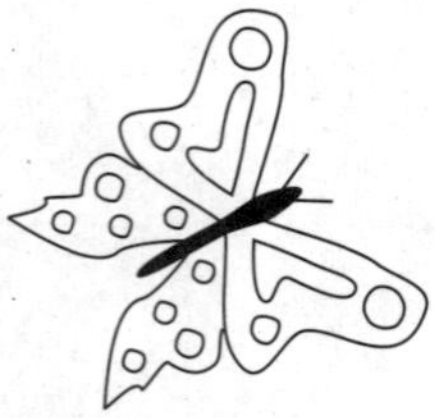 1 body part	 2 body parts	 3 body parts
 4 body parts	 More than 4 body parts	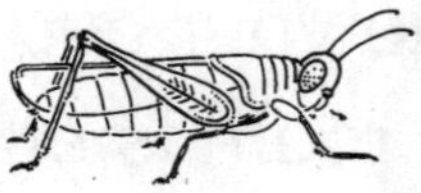 6 legs
 8 legs	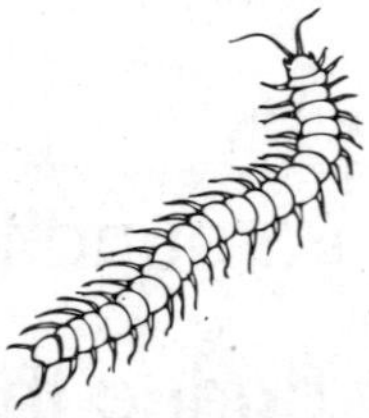 More than 8 legs	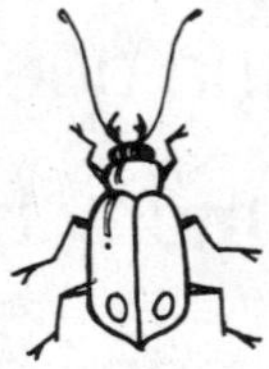 Antennae
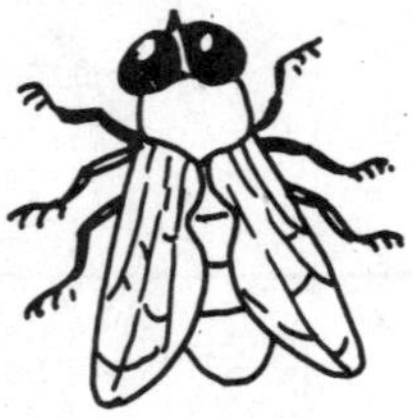 2 wings	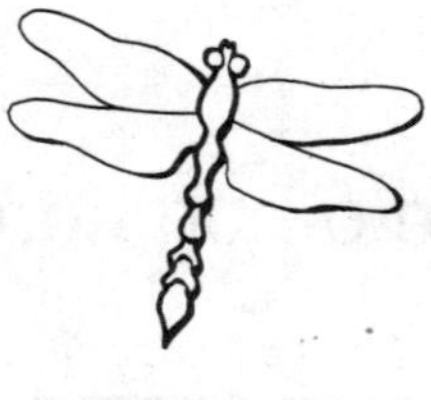 4 wings	 Colorful wings

© Harcourt Achieve Inc. All rights reserved.

Name ______________________ Date ____________

Results

Place a check next to the descriptions that describe your bugs.

Descriptions	Bug 1	Bug 2	Bug 3
1 body part			
2 body parts			
3 body parts			
4 body parts			
More than 4 body parts			
6 legs			
8 legs			
More than 8 legs			
Antennae			
2 wings			
4 wings			
Colorful wings			

Conclusions

Write the answers.

1. List the types of bugs that are in your bottle.

   Bug 1 ______________

   Bug 2 ______________

   Bug 3 ______________

© Harcourt Achieve Inc. All rights reserved.

Name ______________________ Date ____________

2. List three things each of your bugs inherited.

#	Bug 1	Bug 2	Bug 3
1			
2			
3			

Connection to Physical Science

Look at this bug seesaw. Place your three bugs on it in a way that will leave it balanced. Use dots to show the bugs. Assume the three bugs each weigh the same amount.

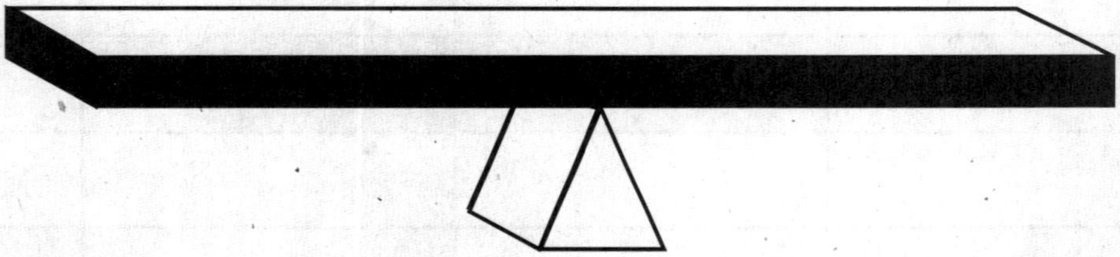

© Harcourt Achieve Inc. All rights reserved.

Name ______________________ Date ____________

Experiment 3: From Mom or Surroundings?

Materials

1 bug per child in a large plastic bottle with air holes

a few leaves, pebbles, and twigs

Purpose Everything about how a bug looks and what a bug does is either inherited or due to the world around it. In this experiment, you will make a list of how a certain bug acts and what it looks like. You will then decide which things on your list are inherited and which are not.

Procedure

1. Drop a few leaves, pebbles, and twigs into the bottle.
2. Watch your bug move around in the plastic bottle.
3. Look at the Results Table. Fill in the second column with facts about your bug.
4. Complete the last column based on your second column facts. Circle the word that describes how a bug looks and what a bug does.

Results

	Facts About Your Bug	Inherited or Due to the World Around It?
Number of legs		Inherited Environment
Number of wings		Inherited Environment
Number of body parts		Inherited Environment
Does it have an antenna?		Inherited Environment
Does it walk around?		Inherited Environment
Does it crawl up the sides of the bottle?		Inherited Environment

© Harcourt Achieve Inc. All rights reserved.

Name ______________________ Date ____________

	Facts About Your Bug	Inherited or Due to the World Around It?
When it is on the bottom of the bottle and comes to the side, does it go up the side?		Inherited Environment
What does it do when it comes to a twig?		Inherited Environment
What does it do when it comes to a pebble?		Inherited Environment
What does it do when it comes to a leaf?		Inherited Environment

Conclusions

Complete the sentences.

1. Some kinds of things that bugs inherit are ______________________

____.

2. Some kinds of things bugs do because of their environment are

____.

Connection to Earth Science

Think about how bugs react to the following weather conditions: windy day, rainy day, sunny day, volcano, flood, cold weather. Choose one type of weather from the list and draw a picture showing the effect on bugs.

© Harcourt Achieve Inc. All rights reserved.

Name ______________________________ Date ______________

Lesson 9: Background

Weather changes each day. Many of these changes are easy to see and understand. You can watch the weather changes to decide what you are going to do each day. You can also watch the weather changes to **predict**, or guess, what will happen with the weather.

Clouds are one thing that can be helpful in predicting weather. It rains when there is a lot of water in the clouds. Clouds with a lot of water are usually dark. Clouds with very little water are white. When a cloud gets too full of water to hold it all, it rains.

Weather reporters use weather **symbols** to tell what the weather will be each day. They might use symbols like these.

Sunny

Partly Cloudy

Cloudy

Rainy

Snowy

If you watch the weather on TV or read about the weather in a newspaper, you will see symbols like these. They are a way of telling what the weather is like by using pictures.

For hundreds of years, people have been watching and measuring weather to help understand it. Some tools are used to measure weather. A **thermometer** measures temperature. A **wind gauge** measures wind speed. A **Beaufort Scale** measures wind speed. A **wind vane** measures direction of wind. A **rain gauge** measures how much rain.

Connection to Physical Science

Explore the idea that a cloud can get too full of water to hold it all. Use a sponge as a cloud and water to demonstrate.

© Harcourt Achieve Inc. All rights reserved.

Name ______________________________ Date ______________

Experiment 1: Weather Chart

Materials

for each 3 children: poster board, pencil, yardstick, marker

Purpose The weather changes from day to day. In this experiment you will study weather changes by making a 30-day weather chart.

Procedure

1. Use the pencil to divide the poster board into six rows and seven columns. Erase and move the marks until you think they look almost even.

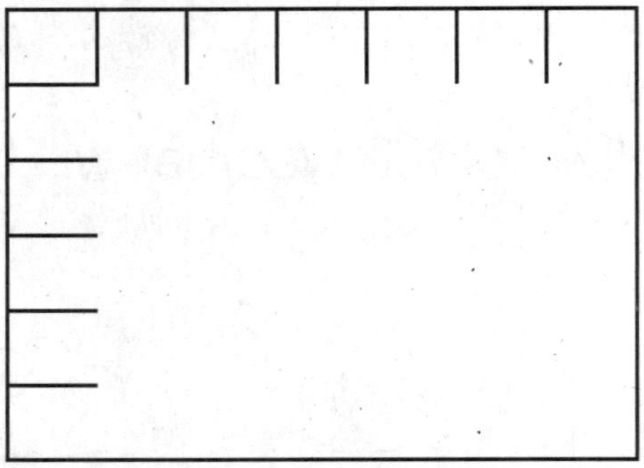

2. Use a marker and the yardstick to draw the lines you have marked out.

3. Beginning with Sunday, write the days of the week in the first row.

S	M	T	W	TH	F	S

4. Beginning with today, write the dates in the corners of the boxes.

© Harcourt Achieve Inc. All rights reserved.

Name ______________________________ Date ______________

5. Look outside each day to decide if the weather is sunny, partly cloudy, cloudy, rainy, or snowy. Copy the picture into the poster for that day.

Sunny

Partly Cloudy

Cloudy

Rainy

Snowy

Results

1. Count the days in your weather chart to fill in this table.

# of Sunny Days	# of Partly Cloudy Days	# of Sunny Days	# of Rainy Days	# of Snowy Days

Conclusions

Circle the correct answer.

1. The 30 days were mostly—
   A. sunny.
   B. partly cloudy.
   C. cloudy.
   D. rainy.
   E. snowy.

Complete each sentence.

2. There were more ____________ days this month than there were ____________ days.
3. There were the least amount of ____________ days than any other type of day.

Connection to Life Science

Would the 30 days in your weather chart have been good days for a garden? Tell why or why not.

© Harcourt Achieve Inc. All rights reserved.

Name ________________________________ Date ________________

Experiment 2: Wind, Rain, or Shine

Materials

adult helper
4 cups of soil
4 cups of sand
4 cups of pebbles
4 cups of rocks
4 cups of cedar mulch
4 cups of water
large balloon (can blow up to be bigger than your head)
watering can with a sprinkle nozzle
heat lamp
15 paper plates
3 plastic bowls

Purpose Rain, wind, and sun affect different things in different ways. You will explore some of these differences in this experiment.

Procedure

1. Divide the water into the 3 bowls. Divide each of the other 5 materials into 3 parts (approximately) and place each part on a paper plate.
2. Place 1 plate and bowl of each material under the heat lamp. This is the "sun" group.
3. Take the other 12 plates and bowls outside. Put one of each type of material on one side of a sidewalk. These materials will all experience "rain." Put the other 6 plates and bowls on the other side of a sidewalk. These materials will all experience "wind."
4. Blow up the balloon and hold the air in with your thumb and finger. Aim the balloon end at one of the plates/bowls in the "wind" group and let the air out.
5. After the plate/bowl has experienced "wind," fill in the matching square in the Results Table.
6. Repeat with the other 5 plates/bowls in the "wind" group.
7. Fill the water can with water. Pour the water on one of the plates/bowls in the "rain" group.
8. After the plate/bowl has experienced "rain," fill in the matching square in the Results Table.
9. Repeat with the other 5 plates/bowls in the "rain" group.
10. After the plates/bowls in the "sun" group have been under the heat lamp for at least an hour, fill in the matching square in the Results Table.

© Harcourt Achieve Inc. All rights reserved.

Name ______________________________ Date ________________

Results

Use the following comments in the table:

- No change
- It scattered or spread out.
- It got hard.
- Some of it seems to be gone.

	What happened when the air from the balloon blew at it?	What happened when the water was poured on it?	What happened after the heat lamp shone on it?
Soil			
Sand			
Pebbles			
Rocks			
Cedar mulch			
Water			

Conclusions

Circle the correct answer.

1. When found on the ground naturally, which material is MOST likely to change by spending a week in the sun?

   A. rocks **B.** cedar mulch **C.** water

2. When found on the ground naturally, which material is LEAST likely to change by a rainy week?

   A. soil **B.** pebbles **C.** rocks

Connection to Life Science

Think about sand on a windy day. Find what the wind has to do with the fact that very few plants grow on a sandy beach.

© Harcourt Achieve Inc. All rights reserved.

Name ______________________ Date ____________

Experiment 3: Beaufort Scale

Purpose The Beaufort Scale has been used for many years to report wind speeds. In this experiment, you will use the scale to report the wind speed for a week.

Materials

adult helper, kindling wood, small grill, matches, a few leaves and twigs, umbrella, flag about 20 inches x 20 inches on a flagpole, 3 small branches, 3 sheets of paper

The Beaufort Scale	
0: Calm. Smoke goes straight up. Wind speed: Less than 1 mph	7: Light gale. Whole large trees swaying. Hard to walk against the wind. Flags straight out. Wind speed: 32–38 mph
1: Light air. Smoke moves a little to the side as it goes up. Wind speed: 1–3 mph	8: Full gale. Twigs break from trees. Cars have trouble staying on road. Hard to walk with the wind. Wind speed: 39–46 mph
2: Light breeze. Can feel wind on skin. Leaves and flags move a little. Wind speed: 4–7 mph	9: Strong gale. Light damage to buildings—Items such as satellite disks and awnings might blow off. Wind speed: 47–54 mph
3: Gentle breeze. Leaves and twigs move constantly. Flags wave gently. Wind speed: 8–12 mph	10: Storm. Trees pulled out of ground. Quite a bit of damage to buildings. Wind speed: 55–63 mph
4: Steady breeze. Paper and dust move on the ground. Wind speed: 13–18 mph	11: Strong storm. Widespread damage. Wind speed: 64–75 mph
5: Fresh breeze. Small trees sway. Flags flap lightly. Wind speed: 19–24 mph	12: Hurricane. Huge amounts of damage. Wind speed: More than 75 mph
6: Strong breeze. Large branches sway. Flags whip. Umbrellas are hard to hold in place. Wind speed: 25–31 mph	

© Harcourt Achieve Inc. All rights reserved.

Name ______________________________ Date ______________

Procedure

1. For one week, use the Beaufort Scale to measure the wind up through Level 8. (Warning: Do not try to measure any winds that are higher than Level 8. It is too dangerous for you to be outside in these winds.)
2. For each day, begin at the left of the Results Table. Answer each question and circle a level or go on.

Results

		Mon	Tues	Wed	Thurs	Fri
Is the wind blowing twigs off the trees? Is it hard to walk with the wind at your back?	If yes, circle Level 8. If not, go on.	Level 8	Level 8	Level 8	Level 8	Level 8
Are whole large trees swaying? Is the flag standing straight out? Is it hard to walk against the wind?	If yes, circle Level 7. If not, go on.	Level 7	Level 7	Level 7	Level 7	Level 7
Are large branches swaying, but not the whole trees? Is the flag whipping about? Is an umbrella hard to hold in place?	If yes, circle Level 6. If not, go on.	Level 6	Level 6	Level 6	Level 6	Level 6
Are small trees swaying, but not large trees or branches? Is the flag flapping lightly?	If yes, circle Level 5. If not, go on.	Level 5	Level 5	Level 5	Level 5	Level 5
Do paper and dust move on the ground, but even small trees are not blowing?	If yes, circle Level 4. If not, go on.	Level 4	Level 4	Level 4	Level 4	Level 4

© Harcourt Achieve Inc. All rights reserved.

Name ______________________ Date ____________

		Mon	Tues	Wed	Thurs	Fri
Are leaves and twigs blowing about, but not dust and paper? Is the flag waving gently?	If yes, circle Level 3. If not, go on.	Level 3	Level 3	Level 3	Level 3	Level 3
Can you feel the wind on your skin, but no leaves or twigs are blowing about? Is the flag moving just a little bit?	If yes, circle Level 2. If not, go on.	Level 2	Level 2	Level 2	Level 2	Level 2
Does smoke move a little to the side as it goes up, but you cannot feel any wind on your skin?	If yes, circle Level 1. If not, go on.	Level 1	Level 1	Level 1	Level 1	Level 1
Does smoke go straight up and the air seems perfectly still?	If yes, circle Level 0.	Level 0	Level 0	Level 0	Level 0	Level 0

Conclusions

Use the Beaufort Scale and your results to fill in this table.

Day	Wind Level
Monday	
Tuesday	
Wednesday	
Thursday	
Friday	

Connection to Life Science

Animals have a natural instinct to protect themselves during storms. They try to hide in safe places. At what level on the Beaufort Scale do you think an ant, a fox, and an elephant would need to find a safe place?

© Harcourt Achieve Inc. All rights reserved.

Name ______________________________ Date ______________

Lesson 10: Background

Earth spins around, or **rotates**, one time every 24 hours. This creates days and nights.

While Earth rotates, it also circles, or **orbits**, the sun. Earth's orbit gives us the four **seasons**: winter, spring, summer, and fall.

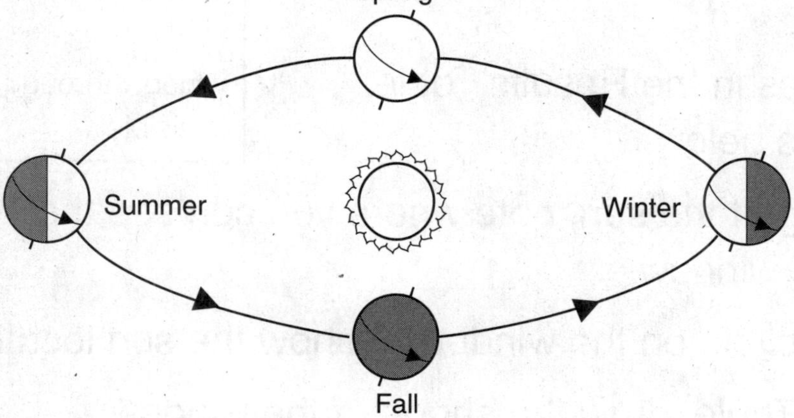

The sun always shines on some part of Earth. You have night when the sun is not shining on your part of Earth. When the sun looks like it is coming up or going down, it is really just Earth turning.

When something is between the sun and the ground, a shadow is created. A **shadow** is a sunless spot the shape of what is blocking the sun. A high sun creates a short shadow and a low sun creates a long shadow.

Shadow A is shorter because the sun is higher up.

Connection to Physical Science

A flag is a solid thing. Is a shadow a solid? If not, what is it?

© Harcourt Achieve Inc. All rights reserved.

Name ______________________________ Date ____________

Experiment 1: Sunny Windows

Materials

adult helper to make sure children do not look at sun

five 5-inch-diameter yellow circles

tape

clock

window through which the sun is visible

Purpose Earth makes one complete turn every 24 hours. As it turns, it makes the sun look like it is moving across the sky from east to west. In this experiment, you will track where you see the sun during the day.

Procedure

At each of the times in the Results Table, complete the steps below.

1. Without looking at the sun, note where you can see the sun by looking out the window.
2. Tape a yellow circle on the window to show the sun location.
3. In the Results Table, draw the shape of the window.
4. In the window you have drawn, draw a circle to show where you have marked the sun on the window.
5. Draw an arrow from the time to the sun position.

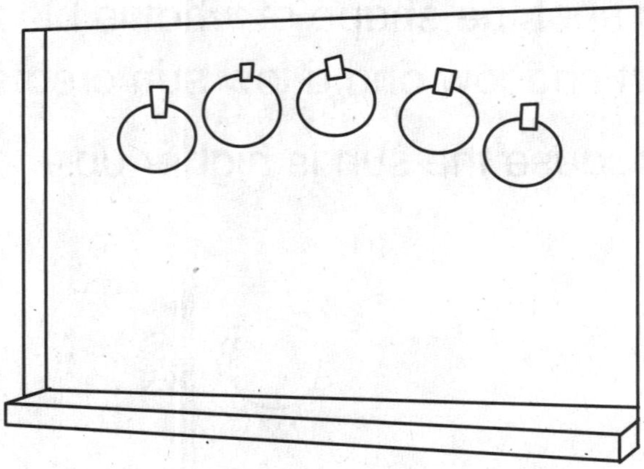

© Harcourt Achieve Inc. All rights reserved.

Name ____________________ Date ____________

Results

9:00 A.M.	11:00 A.M.	12:00 P.M.	1:00 P.M.	3:00 P.M.

(Draw the window. Show where you have marked the sun.)

Conclusions

Circle the word or words that best complete each sentence.

1. In the morning, the sun appears to be (higher, lower) in the sky than at noon.
2. The sun appears to move in a (straight line, curved path).
3 At 3:00 P.M., the sun is in the (east, west).

Connection to Life Science

The sun is most likely to burn people during the hours when it appears highest in the sky. Make a poster asking people to stay out of the sun during the four hours when they are most likely to burn.

© Harcourt Achieve Inc. All rights reserved.

Name ______________________________ Date ____________

Experiment 2: Daily Shadows

Materials

fence post, small tree, or flagpole

tape measure

pencil

Purpose When something is between the sun and the ground, a shadow is created.

Procedure

NOTE: This experiment needs to take place on a sunny day.

1. At each of the times shown in the Results Table, take the tape measure and go out to the fence post, small tree, or flagpole that you are using for this experiment.
2. Measure the length of the shadow given off by the fence post, small tree, or flagpole.
3. Write the measurements in the Results Table next to the correct time.

Results

Time	Length of Shadow
9:00 A.M.	
10:00 A.M.	
11:00 A.M.	
12:00 P.M.	
1:00 P.M.	
2:00 P.M.	
3:00 P.M.	

© Harcourt Achieve Inc. All rights reserved.

Name ______________________ Date ______________

Conclusions

Circle the correct answer.

1. As a day goes along, shadows—
   - **A.** get longer.
   - **B.** get shorter.
   - **C.** get shorter and then get longer.
2. When the sun appears higher in the sky—
   - **A.** shadows are shorter.
   - **B.** shadows are longer.
   - **C.** shadows are easier to find.
3. At what time is the shadow about the same length as the 9:00 A.M. shadow?
   - **A.** 11:00 A.M.
   - **B.** 1:00 P.M.
   - **C.** 3:00 P.M.

Connection to Life Science

Find two types of plants that need to grow in the shade to stay alive.

© Harcourt Achieve Inc. All rights reserved.

Name ____________________________ Date ______________

Experiment 3: A Basketball World

Materials
basketball
flashlight
round sticker

Purpose Every day it looks like the sun moves across the sky from sunup to sundown. But the sun is not really moving. Earth is moving. In this experiment, you will act out Earth moving so you understand how it works.

Procedure

1. Turn the flashlight on and set it on a desk. The flashlight will be the sun.
2. Hold the basketball close enough to the flashlight so that the light beam is smaller than the flashlight and can be easily seen on the basketball. The basketball will be Earth.
3. Slowly turn the basketball around and around. Watch what happens to the light.
4. Place the round sticker on the basketball. The sticker stands for where you live on Earth.
5. Slowly turn the basketball again. Watch what happens to the light.

Results

Answer the questions.

1. What happened to the light from the flashlight as you turned the basketball?

____

2. Once you put the sticker on, was the light always shining on it?

____

© Harcourt Achieve Inc. All rights reserved.

Name ______________________________ Date ______________

Conclusions

Circle the correct answer.

1. People once thought that the sun moved and Earth stood still because—

   A. they were silly people, and they were not really paying attention.

   B. when you stand on Earth, you can't tell you are moving, and it looks like the sun is moving.

   C. the sun used to move.

2. If you watch the sticker, you can see how day and night work. It is night where the sticker is when—

   A. the light is not on the sticker at all.

   B. the light is shining sideways at the sticker.

   C. the light is shining straight at the sticker.

3. When it is night where you live, the sun is—

   A. shining straight at your area.

   B. on the other side of the world.

   C. not shining at all.

Connection to Life Science

Think what would happen if the world stopped turning. Wherever you are when it stops is where you would always be. On another sheet of paper, draw a picture showing where you would want to be in relation to the sun. On the back of your picture, write a paragraph telling why you picked this place.

© Harcourt Achieve Inc. All rights reserved.

Name ______________________ Date ____________

Lesson 11: Background

Things found on Earth are rocks, soils, water, and gases.

A **rock** is a hard, nonliving thing that can be very big to very small in size. Big rocks can be mountain-sized to hill-sized to people-sized. Any rock that is hard to lift could be called a big rock.

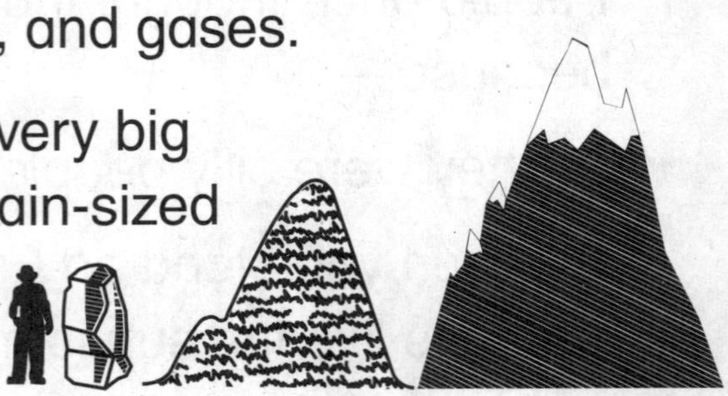

Little rocks are rocks that you can lift. They are bigger than pebbles. Scientists say that a pebble is any rock that is smaller than $2\frac{1}{2}$ inches around. But most people think of pebbles as rocks that are as big as those shown here.

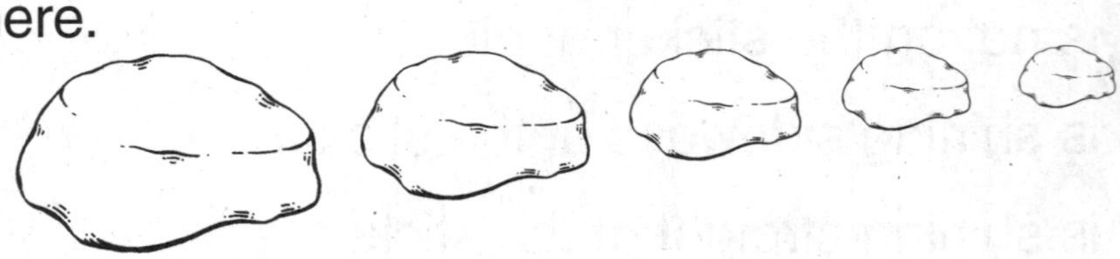

When a pebble breaks up, it turns into sand, dirt, or silt. Dirt is like soil. It is made up of finely crushed rock and plants and animals that are broken down. **Silt** is fine dirt that is carried by moving water. Silt usually ends up on the bottom or sides of a body of water, such as a lake.

Water helps break rocks down into pebbles, soil, sand, and silt. Water can break rock down by slapping against it and by throwing it against other rocks. Water can also change the looks of other materials, such as many foods. Since water can change foods, it is often mixed with foods.

Connection to Physical Science

If you get hit with a rock, it hurts! But it doesn't hurt to get hit with water. Even little children think it is fun to play in sprinklers. So, if rocks hurt and water doesn't, how can water break up rocks? With the help of an adult, put a grilling charcoal in a colander under a steady stream of water for five to ten minutes. Watch to see how a steady stream of water that doesn't hurt you can break up something hard.

© Harcourt Achieve Inc. All rights reserved.

Name ______________________ Date ____________

Experiment 1: Water, Dirt, Air, and Plastic

Purpose Some foods change when put in dirt, soaked in water, put out in the air, or wrapped in plastic. In this experiment, you will explore some of these changes.

Materials

- bowl of water
- planter of dirt
- paper plate
- plastic wrap
- four pieces of lettuce
- four $\frac{1}{4}$-cup bowls of northern beans
- four apple slices
- four 1-tablespoon pieces of butter

Procedure

1. Place one piece of lettuce, the beans from one bowl, one apple slice, and one tablespoon of butter in the bowl of water.
2. Stir the mixture for 5 minutes.
3. Record your results in the Results Table.
4. Place one piece of lettuce, the beans from one bowl, one apple slice, and one tablespoon of butter in four separate holes in the planter of dirt.
5. Cover the materials with dirt.
6. Leave the planter alone for three weeks.
7. Dig up the materials and record the results in the Results Table.
8. Place one piece of lettuce, the beans from one bowl, one apple slice, and one tablespoon of butter on the paper plate in the open air of the room.
9. Leave the materials on the plate for one week.
10. Record your results in the Results Table.
11. Place one piece of lettuce, the beans from one bowl, one apple slice, and one tablespoon of butter in the plastic wrap.
12. Leave the materials in the plastic wrap for one week.
13. Record the results in the Results Table.

© Harcourt Achieve Inc. All rights reserved.

Name ______________________ Date ______________

Results

	What did the lettuce look like?	What did the beans look like?	What did the apple slices look like?	What did the butter look like?
Bowl of water				
Planter of dirt				
Paper plate				
Plastic wrap				

Conclusions

Write Water, Dirt, Air, or Plastic.

1. Which is most likely to cause food to dry out? ______________
2. Which is most likely to cause foods to quickly fall apart?

   ____
3. Which is most likely to trap water and cause some foods to turn moldy? ______________
4. Which is most likely to cause some foods to slowly fall apart?

   ____

Connection to Life Science

Look to find a living thing that can live in water, a living thing that cannot live in water, a living thing that can live in dirt, and a living thing that cannot live in dirt. Share what you find with a friend.

© Harcourt Achieve Inc. All rights reserved.

Name ______________________ Date ____________

Experiment 2: Washing with Water

Purpose Water can remove some spills from clothing. Water and soap can remove others. In this experiment, you will make a mess so you can find out what water can do!

Materials

sink or two tubs of water (one for non-soapy rinsing and one for soapy rinsing)

dish soap

per child: unstained white cotton 8 inch x 8 inch T-shirt fabric

1 teaspoon of mustard

1 teaspoon of ketchup

1 teaspoon of mud

1 teaspoon of wet sand

1 teaspoon of chocolate

1 teaspoon of coleslaw

1 teaspoon of caramel

1 teaspoon melted cheese

8 plastic spoons

permanent black marker

paper plate

Procedure and Results

1. Use the black marker to write the names of the smear materials on the cloth as shown.

2. Place a dab of each smear material under the name. Keeping it under the name, smear it around.

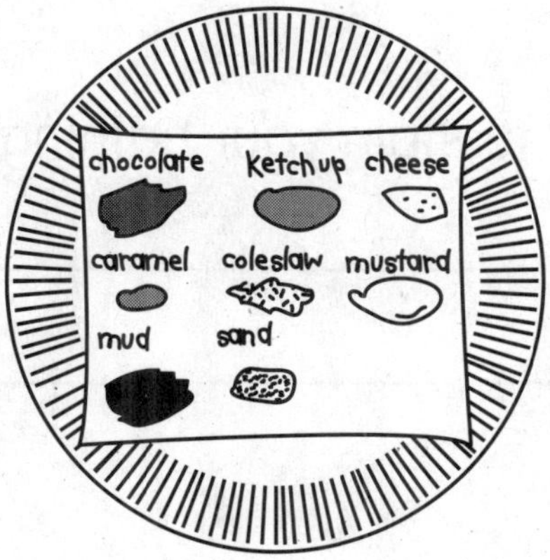

3. Wash the cloth in plain water for about one minute. Rub quite a bit to try to remove the smear.

© Harcourt Achieve Inc. All rights reserved.

Name ______________________________ Date ______________

4. Use the black marker to note which smear materials washed out with water. Write a W where the smear was.
5. Squirt dish soap on the cloth. Rub the cloth very hard to try and get the smears out.
6. Use the black marker to note which smear materials washed out with soap. Write an S where the smear was.
7. Do not write anything on the smears that still show after you scrubbed them with soap. You will know what they are by the stain.

Conclusions

Circle the correct answer.

1. Which of the following is LEAST likely to wash out?

   A. sauces made with tomatoes

   B. sauces made with dirt

   C. sauces made with cheese

2. Which of the following would you LEAST want to spill on a good shirt?

   A. mustard **B.** coleslaw **C.** chocolate

Answer the questions.

3. Based on your results, would you expect to stain your bathing suit at the beach? Tell why. ______________________________

   ____

Connection to Life Science

Besides being helpful in keeping our clothes clean, water has many other uses. List five ways that water is helpful to plants, people, and other animals.

© Harcourt Achieve Inc. All rights reserved.

Name ______________________________ Date ______________

Experiment 3: Rocks to Pebbles to Sand to Silt

Purpose Rocks break down to pebbles, sand, and silt. In this experiment, you will line up rocks, pebbles, sand grains, and silt grains from largest to smallest.

Materials

container with rocks, pebbles, sand, and silt (The largest measurement of the biggest rock should be about 2 inches.)

tweezers

Procedure

1. From the container, choose ten items that fit into the Results Boxes.
2. Use tweezers to pick up items that are too small to pick up with your fingers.

Results

Rocks

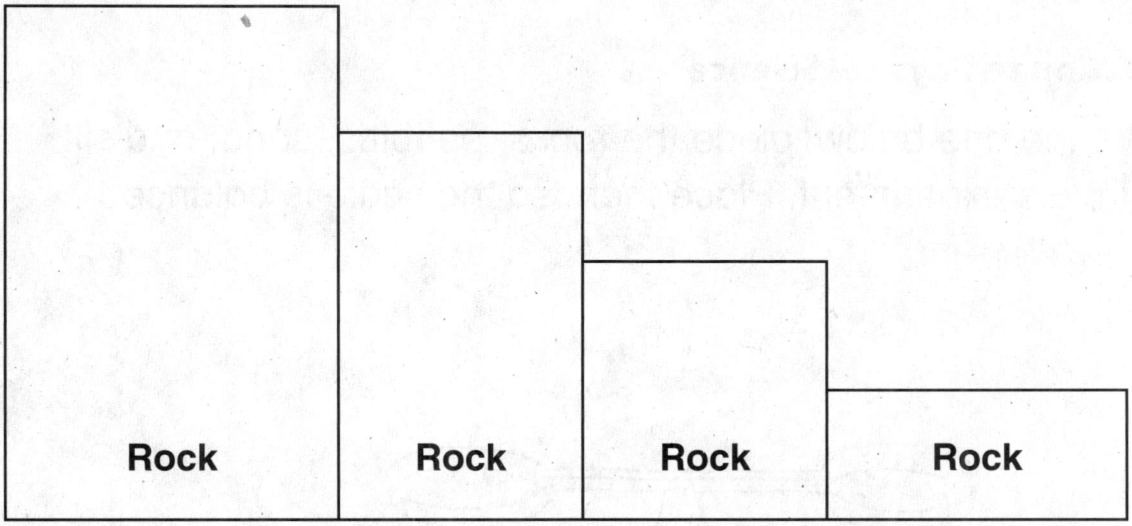

Pebbles

Sand

Silt

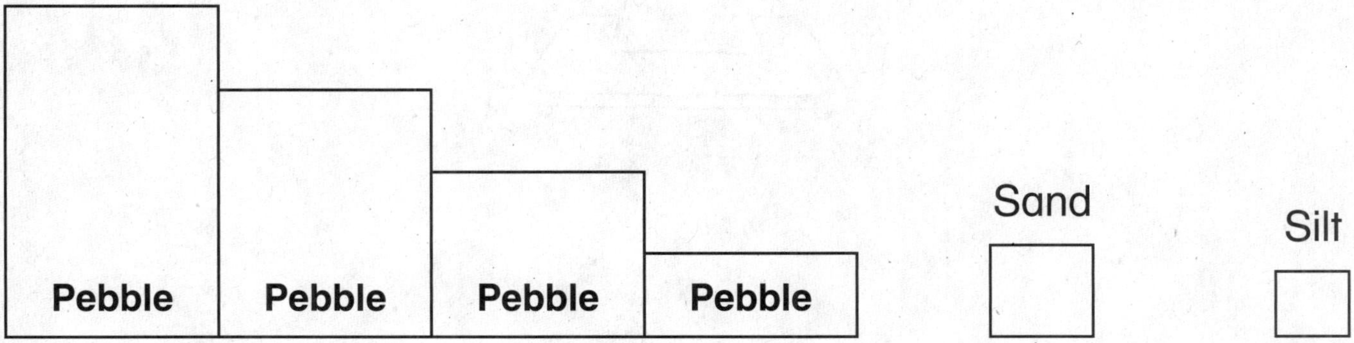

© Harcourt Achieve Inc. All rights reserved.

Name ______________________ Date ______________

Conclusions

Answer the questions.

1. What is the difference between a rock and a pebble? ______________________

____

2. What is the difference between a rock and sand? ______________________

____

3. What is the difference between sand and silt? ______________________

____

4. How can you tell a small rock from a pebble? ______________________

____

Connection to Physical Science

On a scale like the one below, place the rocks, pebbles, sand, and silt you lined up in this experiment. Place them so the scale is balanced.

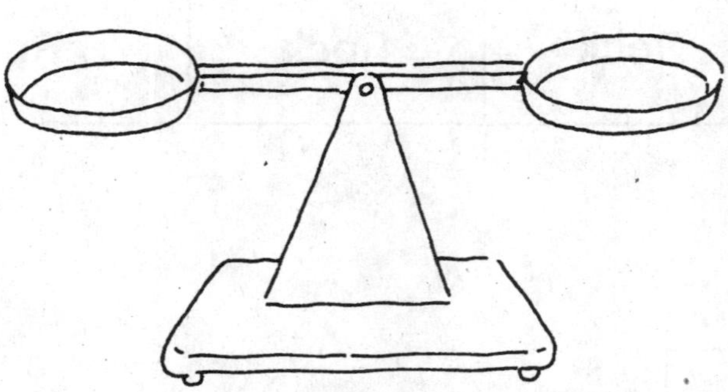

© Harcourt Achieve Inc. All rights reserved.

Name ______________________________ Date ______________

Lesson 12: Background

Have you ever heard someone say, “Oh, it’s just dirt!”? When you hear this, you might think that dirt is not very important. But dirt is important in many ways.

You would not have food if it were not for dirt!
Most plants we eat, like lettuce and carrots, grow in dirt. Animals we eat, like cows and chickens, also eat plants that grow in dirt.

You would not have clothes if it were not for dirt!
Many clothes are made with plant and animal parts. For example, cotton is grown from plants and is used to make clothes like T-shirts.

You would not be living in your home if it were not for dirt!
Wood is made from living trees that grow in dirt. Brick can be made from dirt. Wood and bricks are used to build houses.

Connection to Life Science

Find out the steps from a seed being planted to a plant becoming part of a rock. Write the steps in sequence.

© Harcourt Achieve Inc. All rights reserved.

Name ______________________________ Date ______________

Experiment 1: Dirt Shakes

Purpose You will explore three dirt facts: Dirt is made up of different things. Dirt samples from two different places are usually different. Dirt on top of the ground is different from dirt that is deeper in the ground.

Materials

9 plastic jars with screw-on lids (such as empty large peanut butter, mayonnaise, or mixed nuts jars)

water

magnifying glass

9 self-stick labels

from 3 different places: $\frac{1}{2}$ cup of topsoil, $\frac{1}{2}$ cup of subsoil, and $\frac{1}{2}$ cup of deep soil

Procedure

1. Make three labels with the name of each location. On one of each of the three labels, write Topsoil, Subsoil, and Deep soil under the location.

Sample Labels:

Soccer field Topsoil	Soccer field Subsoil	Soccer field Deep soil

2. Stick the labels on the plastic jars.
3. Fill the jars with water to about one inch from the top.
4. Place the lids on the jars.
5. Shake the jars for 2 minutes.
6. Let the jars stand for about 2 hours.
7. Use the magnifying glass to look at the layers through the jar walls.
8. Complete the Results Table.

Results

	How many different layers do you see in the jar?	Which layer is the darkest? (top, middle, bottom)	Which layer is made up of the largest pieces?
Location: ____________ Topsoil			
Location: ____________ Subsoil			

© Harcourt Achieve Inc. All rights reserved.

Name ______________________________ Date ______________

Location: ________ **Deep Soil**			
Location: ________ **Topsoil**			
Location: ________ **Subsoil**			
Location: ________ **Deep Soil**			
Location: ________ **Topsoil**			
Location: ________ **Subsoil**			
Location: ________ **Deep Soil**			

Conclusions

Complete each sentence.

1. One thing that is the same in all the bottom layers is ______________.
2. One thing that is different about some of the top layers is __________.
3. One thing that is different about the deep-soil jars is ______________.

Connection to Life Science

On a sheet of paper, make a cartoon showing a plant talking about topsoil, subsoil, and/or deep soil.

© Harcourt Achieve Inc. All rights reserved.

Name ______________________ Date ____________

Experiment 2: Sifting Through the Dirt

Purpose Dirt is made up of different-sized pieces. In this experiment, you will separate dirt into different-sized pieces and study the different sizes.

Materials

bucket of dirt

3 different-sized grid sifter screens (approx. hole sizes: $\frac{1}{4}$-inch square, $\frac{1}{2}$-inch square, and 1-inch square)

newspapers

Procedure

1. Spread newspapers out in four different areas.
2. Place each of the three grids on one of the newspaper spreads.
3. Pour the dirt on the smallest grid.
4. Pick the grid up and shake it until dirt stops falling onto the newspaper.
5. Pour the remaining dirt from the small grid onto the middle-sized grid.
6. Pick up the middle-sized grid and shake it until dirt stops falling onto the newspaper.
7. Pour the remaining dirt from the middle-sized grid onto the large-sized grid.
8. Pick up the large-sized grid and shake it until dirt stops falling onto the newspaper.
9. Place the large-sized grid and any remaining dirt that is on it onto the newspaper spread that has not been used.
10. Complete the Results Table.

© Harcourt Achieve Inc. All rights reserved.

Name ______________________________ Date ______________

Results

Describe what fell onto the news-paper from the smallest grid.	Describe what fell onto the news-paper from the middle-sized grid.	Describe what fell onto the news-paper from the large-sized grid.	Describe what was too large to fall through even the large-sized grid.

Conclusions

Circle the correct answer.

1. There are more non-soil things on—
   - **A.** the small-grid newspaper.
   - **B.** the middle-sized-grid newspaper.
   - **C.** the large-grid newspaper.

Answer the questions.

2. What three different things help to make up this dirt?

   ____

3. What surprised you the most about what you saw when you sorted the dirt?

   ____

   ____

Connection to Life Science

On a sheet of paper, draw a web like the one below. Fill in your web to tell how soil is involved with live and dead plants and animals.

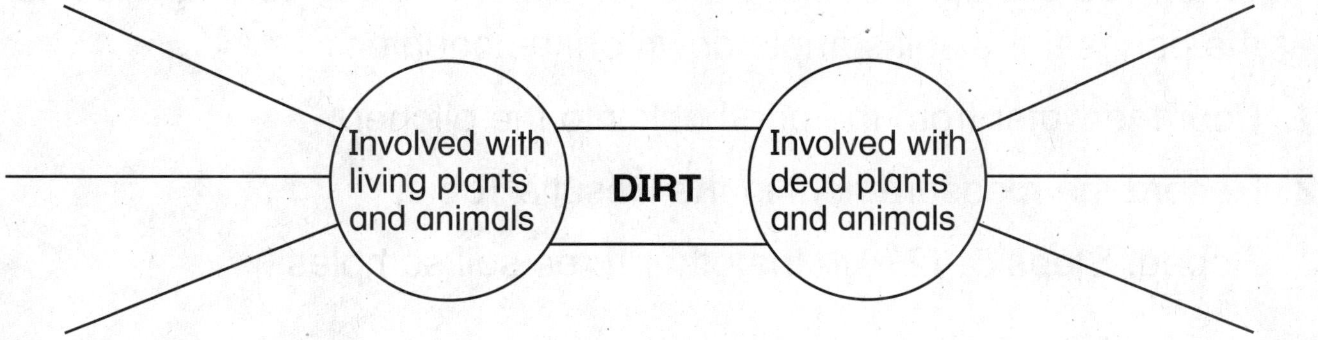

© Harcourt Achieve Inc. All rights reserved.

Name ______________________________ Date ______________

Experiment 3: Finding Thirsty Soil

Materials

four 2-liter soda bottles with the slanted tops cut off

about 4 cups of four different soil types (such as yard soil, riverbed soil, gardening soil, sand, clay, mostly rock soil)

2 aluminum pans

2-quart pitcher with measurements on the sides

water

permanent marker

paper towels

Purpose Rain is needed for plants to grow. In this experiment, you will find how different soils handle rain differently.

Procedure

1. Poke many small holes in the bottoms of the soda bottles so water can easily drain out. Make the holes small enough that the dirt will not fall out.
2. Fill each bottle about half full of one of the four types of soil.
3. Label each soil type by writing on the jug with the marker.
4. Fill the pitchers with 8 cups of water.
5. Hold one of the soil sample bottles over an aluminum pan. Very slowly pour the pitcher of water onto the soil.
6. When you are finished pouring and the water has quit coming out into the pan, set the soil sample down on a paper towel.
7. Pour the water from the pan back into the pitcher.
8. Record the measurement in the Results Table.
9. Again, hold the soil sample bottle over the aluminum pan. Very slowly pour the remaining water onto the soil again.
10. When you are done pouring and the water has quit coming out into the pan, set the soil sample down on the counter.
11. Pour the water from the pan back into the pitcher.
12. Record the measurement in the Results Table.
13. Repeat Steps 5–12 with the other three soil samples.

© Harcourt Achieve Inc. All rights reserved.

Name ______________________________ Date ______________

Results

Fill in the soil samples to match the bottle labels.

	First water pouring (in cup measure-ments)	Second water pouring (in cup measure-ments)	Starting amount of water	Total amount of first and second pourings	Total water soaked up
Soil Sample: ______________			8 cups −		=
Soil Sample: ______________			8 cups −		=
Soil Sample: ______________			8 cups −		=
Soil Sample: ______________			8 cups −		=

Conclusions

Answer the questions.

1. Which type of soil held the most water after the first pouring?

    ____

2. Which type of soil held the most total water? ______________________

3. Which type of soil do you think would be the best for a garden? Tell why.

    ____

    ____

Connection to Life Science

Make a list of the plants that grow in each of the soil types you used in this experiment. Discuss whether the amounts of water the different soils can hold have anything to do with the plants that grow there.

© Harcourt Achieve Inc. All rights reserved.

Name ______________________________ Date ______________

Lab Sheet

Experiment: ______________________________

Purpose:
Observations:
Results:
Conclusions:

© Harcourt Achieve Inc. All rights reserved.

Glossary

balance (p. 21) to place equal weight on either side of a center point

Beaufort Scale (p. 63) a list of wind descriptions that are used to identify wind speeds

camouflage (p. 56) hiding by trying to blend into surroundings

cave (p. 42) a large, dark hole in the ground or the side of a hill or mountain

clouds (p. 63) white or gray objects in the air that are made of tiny drops of water

compare (p. 21) to show how something is the same as or different from another thing

decay (p. 14) to rot or fall apart

Earth (p. 71) the third planet from the sun where humans live

energy (p. 42) the ability to cause change

environment (p. 49) the living and nonliving things in a place

evaporate (p. 14) to change from a liquid into a gas

force (p. 28) a push or a pull

forest (p. 42) a place on Earth that has many trees

gas (p. 14) matter that does not have its own size or shape

habitat (p. 42) a natural place where a plant or animal lives

inherit (p. 56) to receive a characteristic from a parent

liquid (p. 14) matter that has a set size but takes the shape of its container

living thing (p. 35) something that is alive, and grows and changes

mass (p. 7) the amount of matter in an object

matter (p. 7) anything that has mass and takes up space; everything around you

microscope (p. 42) a tool that makes very tiny things look bigger

mixture (p. 14) mixed or blended materials

nature (p. 7) the outside world as it naturally exists

needs (p. 42) what living things must have to live

nonliving (p. 28) something that is not alive, and does not grow and change

orbit (p. 71) a path of an object around another object

© Harcourt Achieve Inc. All rights reserved.

photosynthesis (p. 42) the process by which plants use the sun, air, and water to make food

predict (p. 63) to guess

property (p. 7) a trait that can describe matter

rain gauge (p. 63) a container for measuring how much rain fell

react (p. 49) to act or behave in a certain way

rock (p. 78) a hard, nonliving thing found in nature

root (p. 42) the part of a plant under the ground that takes water and food from the soil

rotate (p. 71) to spin around

scent (p. 49) a smell

season (p. 71) a time of the year; winter, summer, spring, fall

senses (p. 49) smelling, touching, seeing, tasting, and hearing

shadow (p. 71) a patch of shade made when an object is between the rays of the sun and the ground

silt (p. 78) very fine dirt or sand that is carried by rivers

soil (p. 42) loose material that plants need to grow

solid (p. 14) matter that has its own shape and size

stem (p. 42) the main part of a plant

stomata (p. 42) tiny holes that let leaves take in air

sun (p. 42) the closest star to Earth

symbol (p. 63) a thing, such as a small picture, that stands for something else

thermometer (p. 63) a tool to find out how hot or cold it is

trial and error (p. 26) the process of trying over and over until it works

weather (p. 63) the state of the outdoors, such as hot, cold, windy, rainy, snowy, sunny

weight (p. 28) the amount of Earth's pull on an object

wind gauge (p. 63) a tool for measuring wind speed

wind vane (p. 63) a spinning device used to tell wind direction

© Harcourt Achieve Inc. All rights reserved.

Answer Key

This answer key includes answers to the Conclusions only. It is important to note that the children's answers may vary, depending on their experiment results. Science experiments are not always predictable. Use your best judgment when checking answers.

Lesson 1 Experiment 1

Is It Green, Square, or Round?, p. 9

Table and 1–3: Answers will vary but should properly fit into the identified groups.

Lesson 1 Experiment 2

Sorting Objects by Descriptions, p. 11

1. Answers will vary.
2. Answers will vary.
3. Material; explanations will vary but should include that some materials could be harmed by the weather and others would be fine.
4. Size; explanations will vary but should include that large items would not fit into a small box.

Lesson 1 Experiment 3

What Is It Made Of?, p. 13

1. Paper would not be strong enough or hold up very well when used for eating.
2. It would not be strong enough not to break off in the keyhole or to maintain the key notches correctly.
3. It would not be strong enough to last.

Lesson 2 Experiment 1

From Liquid to Solid to Gas, p. 16

1. solids
2. liquids
3. gas
4. solid

Lesson 2 Experiment 2

Hot and Cold Mixing, p. 18

1. easier
2. grapes
3. one thing with no pieces showing

Lesson 2 Experiment 3

Covered with Dirt, p. 20

1. C
2. A

Lesson 3 Experiment 1

Bigger Than the Thing Behind It, p. 23

1. A
2. C
3. B

Lesson 3 Experiment 2

Pencil Balance, p. 25

1. centers
2. eraser end

Lesson 3 Experiment 3

Tower Balance, pp. 26–27

1. The base with four cups should be circled.
2. does not
3. does not
4. do
5. bottom and top
6. is still important
7. Yes, because it has a well-balanced base.
8. all the levels are balanced
9. the bottom three
10. yes
11. balanced
12. Answers will vary.
13. Answers will vary.

Lesson 4 Experiment 1

Moving a Little and a Lot, p. 30

1. hitting
2. moves farther and faster

Lesson 4 Experiment 2

Weight Matters, p. 32

1. A
2. C
3. A

Lesson 4 Experiment 3

It's All in How You Hit It!, p. 34

1. One hand, no swing OR One hand, little swing
2. One hand, big swing OR Two hands, little swing

Lesson 5 Experiment 1

Matching Leaves, p. 37

Table: Answers will vary.
Most likely answer: do

Lesson 5 Experiment 2

Growing Mixed Plants, p. 39

1. cannot
2. can

Lesson 5 Experiment 3

Growing Apple Tree Leaves, p. 41

1. C
2. A

Lesson 6 Experiment 1

Coloring Flowers, p. 44

1. C
2. A
3. The plain water has no food coloring, and the flower does not change colors.

Lesson 6 Experiment 2

A Fight for Light, p. 47

1. A regular bean plant grows straight up.
2. The plant changed directions twice to grow in the direction of the light.
3. The plant might have grown a little bit, but it would probably have died before getting more than an inch or two high.

Lesson 6 Experiment 3

Air Control, p. 48

B

Lesson 7 Experiment 1

Ladybug World, p. 51

1. Answer will depend on experiment results.
2. Answer will depend on experiment results.
3. Answer will depend on experiment results.

Lesson 7 Experiment 2

Mealworm Run, p. 53

1. Answer will depend on experiment results.
2. Answer will depend on experiment results.
3. Answer will depend on experiment results.

Lesson 7 Experiment 3

Smelling Who It Is, p. 55

1. With human smelling abilities, recognizing people completely by smell would require that you get quite close to a person before you recognized him or her. Also, since people often do not detect slight smell variations, people would likely make a lot of identification mistakes if they relied on smell to recognize people.
2. C
3. A

© Harcourt Achieve Inc. All rights reserved.

Lesson 8 Experiment 1

Hiding Insects, p. 57

1. Answers will vary but will likely include a reference to the like colors between bug and background.
2. Answers will vary but will likely include a reference to unlike colors between bug and background.

Lesson 8 Experiment 2

Counting Legs and Body Parts, pp. 59–60

1. Answers will vary.
2. Answers will vary but will likely include characteristics such as number of legs, number of body parts, number or description of wings, and whether or not the insect has antennae.

Lesson 8 Experiment 3

From Mom or Surroundings?, p. 62

1. Answers will vary but should include a reference to how bugs look and how bugs move.
2. Answers will vary but should include a reference to where bugs decide to walk and when bugs decide to turn in a new direction when walking.

Lesson 9 Experiment 1

Weather Chart, p. 65

1. Answers will depend on weather chart results.
2. Answers will depend on weather chart results.
3. Answers will depend on weather chart results.

Lesson 9 Experiment 2

Wind, Rain, or Shine, p. 67

1. C
2. C

Lesson 9 Experiment 3

Beaufort Scale, p. 70

Answers will vary but should include wind speeds (from the Beaufort Scale) that coordinate with the level choices students have indicated.

Lesson 10 Experiment 1

Sunny Windows, p. 73

1. lower
2. curved path
3. west

Lesson 10 Experiment 2

Daily Shadows, p. 75

1. C
2. A
3. C

Lesson 10 Experiment 3

A Basketball World, p. 77

1. B
2. A
3. B

Lesson 11 Experiment 1

Water, Dirt, Air, and Plastic, p. 80

1. air
2. water
3. plastic
4. dirt

Lesson 11 Experiment 2

Washing with Water, p. 82

1. A
2. A
3. No, because sand easily washes out with water.

Lesson 11 Experiment 3

Rocks to Pebbles to Sand to Silt, p. 84

1. Rocks are bigger.
2. Rocks are bigger.
3. Sand grains are bigger.
4. A small rock and a pebble are really the same thing. People subjectively determine if an item is a rock or a pebble.

Lesson 12 Experiment 1

Dirt Shakes, p. 87

1. Answers will vary but might include that the largest, heavier particles are in the bottom layers.
2. Answers will vary but might include that some are darker than others.
3. Answers will vary but might include that the bottom, rocky layer is bigger.

Lesson 12 Experiment 2

Sifting Through the Dirt, p. 89

1. Answers will depend on experiment results.
2. Answers will vary but might likely include responses such as rocks, plant parts, soil, and clay.
3. Answers will vary.

Lesson 12 Experiment 3

Finding Thirsty Soil, p. 91

1. Answer will depend on experiment results.
2. Answer will depend on experiment results.
3. Answer will depend on experiment results.

© Harcourt Achieve Inc. All rights reserved.